Editor
Eric Migliaccio

Editorial Project Manager
Ina Massler Levin, M.A.

Editor in Chief
Sharon Coan, M.S. Ed.

Illustrator
Sue Fullam

Cover Artist
Denise Bauer

Art Coordinator
Denice Adorno

Creative Director
Elayne Roberts

Imaging
James Edward Grace

Product Manager
Phil Garcia

Publishers
Rachelle Cracchiolo, M.S. Ed.
Mary Dupuy Smith, M.S. Ed.

Standards: Meeting Them in the Classroom

Intermediate

Compiled by

J. L. Smith

Teacher Created Materials, Inc.
6421 Industry Way
Westminster, CA 92683
www.teachercreated.com
©*2000 Teacher Created Materials, Inc.*
Reprinted, 2000
Made in U.S.A.
ISBN-1-57690-776-7

Table of Contents

Introduction

The current attention to and concern about the performance of our schools and students is perhaps unprecedented in the history of this country. Presidents, politicians, teachers, educational organizations, and parents have raised questions about the performance of our schools and the performance of our students. The past decade has found these various groups united in their support for holding all students to "high standards" in challenging subject matter.

Holding all students to high standards means rethinking how we can determine whether schools, teachers, and students are achieving at this high level. It means rethinking what is taught and the manner in which we assess what is learned. It means examining how future teachers are educated and how professional staff development is offered to current teachers.

These initiatives, all connected under standards-based instruction, are far beyond the scope of this book. Our focus here is much narrower. We choose here to focus on the learning activities which teachers require to promote and assess learning, and we seek to link these learning activities directly to high standards of achievement. With virtually every state having published its own standards and virtually every subject area now with its own lists—and national standards as an overlay as well—where does one turn for some synthesis of this whole?

Despite their great diversity, there is a surprising level of commonality among these various sources; we have elected to use the collection of standards synthesized by John S. Kendall and Robert J. Marzano in their book entitled *Content Knowledge: A Compendium of Standards and Benchmarks for K–12 Education* * as illustrative of what students at various grade levels should know and be able to do. This book is published jointly by McREL (Mid-continent Regional Educational Laboratory, Inc.— Telephone: 303-337-0990; Web site: *http://www.mcrel.org/*) and ASCD (Association for Supervision and Curriculum Development—Telephone: 1-800-933-2723; Web site: *http://www.ascd.org*).

What is offered in this book are selected samples of subject matter standards and benchmarks. We then provide a rich reservoir of instructional activities which the teacher can easily apply in his/her own classroom as he/she seeks to assist students in successfully mastering the standards outlined.

Our intent is not to be complete in outlining the standards and benchmarks for all subject areas, nor to engage in the dialogue on standards-based instruction. Rather, we seek to assist very busy teachers by providing a rich supply of classroom activities, tied directly to specific standards and benchmarks, and illustrate how these activities can serve as the means to a higher end.

(Note: If a reader/teacher does not have access to the standards for his/her local area, he/she can contact McREL, the appropriate state Department of Education, the subject area professional organizations, or the local central offices of education in his/her city.)

* Kendall, John S., Marzano, Robert J. (1997). *Content Knowledge: A Compendium of Standards and Benchmarks for K–12 Education*, 2nd ed. Aurora, CO: McREL. Used by permission of McREL.

How to Use This Book

Included in this book are examples of activities at the intermediate level for each curricular area: language arts, social studies, math, science, and the arts. In addition to the activity, each page indicates a curricular area and standard; the book itself is divided by curricular area. To identify the curricular area, check the information at the top of each page. The standard each activity meets is also listed at the top of each page. The standards provided in this book are based on a compilation of standards from various organizations and states. The wording of the standard for each activity may not match exactly the wording of the standards you are using. You may have to compare your standards with each activity to find a match.

Provided at the end of this book are two additional sections which take a look at teaching methods and assessment. The section on teaching methods (beginning on page 84) shows how current classroom practices can be directly linked with standards. The assessment section (beginning on page 105) provides ideas for assessing standards and keeping records of student achievement.

A Word About the Activities

Completion of an activity does not mean that a student has demonstrated competency of a standard or benchmark; rather, it provides a student with background, experience, practice, and/or exposure to a standard or a benchmark. Determining student competence in a standard and benchmark is directly tied to assessment. Some standards and benchmarks may be easily assessed after completing several activities. For example, after completing a unit involving standards-based activities on energy, a teacher could assess student understanding of energy types, sources, and conversions and their relationship to heat and temperature. Other standards and benchmarks may need ongoing assessment throughout the year. An example of this would be standards and benchmarks involving the writing process. A standard stating, "Demonstrates competence in the general skills and strategies of the writing process" requires ongoing activities and opportunities for the student in order to demonstrate competence in this standard. One or two activities would not be sufficient. The assessment section provides ways to assess and track each student's demonstration of standards and benchmarks.

An activity does not have to address the entire standard or benchmark to be a worthwhile experience for your students. For some of the standards, addressing the entire standard with one activity is not even a remote possibility. For example, a social studies benchmark states, "Knows the ways that families long ago expressed and transmitted their beliefs and values through oral tradition, literature, song, art, religion, community celebrations, mementos, food, and language." Obviously, one activity will not provide students with enough information or experience to demonstrate the depth implied in this standard. This standard will be met through a number of readings and standards-based activities. Similarly, provided in this book are activities which may meet one portion of a standard. This does not make the activity less valuable. Rather, it provides for a more focused, in-depth look at a portion of the standard.

Consider Multiple Intelligences

Gardner's Theory on Multiple Intelligences reminds us that students learn differently. When selecting activities in relation to standards, be aware of the various intelligences represented by the students in your class. The kind of rich environment that nurtures crystallizing experiences is particularly important for young children because it gives them such an early start. Nevertheless, older children, as well as adults, can also benefit from this kind of environment. Think of someone like Grandma Moses who was exposed to painting very late in life and became famous for her work in that medium.

Teachers should endeavor to infuse the intelligences into activities and lessons. However, selecting activities which both cover the intelligences and meet standards can be tricky. The activities and lessons need to provide meaningful ways to address standards. Some of the intelligences are easier to infuse than others, and some curricular areas are easier to manipulate. Most social studies lessons lend themselves nicely to the infusion approach. Using a standard from United States history, your lesson plan might look something like this:

Standard: Understands the causes and nature of movements of large groups of people into and within the United States, now and long ago
Benchmark: Understands the experience of immigrant groups

Synopsis of Lesson: Over the period of a week (or longer, if necessary), students will review material and complete the following:

- meet together in cooperative groups to develop strategies for remembering the various immigrant groups studied. (*Interpersonal*)

- design and create a mural showing what an immigrant might have seen as his or her boat was arriving in New York Harbor. (*Visual/Spatial*)

- learn a song that is representative of an immigrant group's culture. (*Musical/Rhythmic*)

- learn a dance that is representative of an immigrant group's culture. (*Bodily/Kinesthetic*)

- gather data about numbers of immigrants during specific time periods, and then organize the data in a graph. (*Logical/Mathematical*)

- reflect on the experience of an immigrant. (*Intrapersonal*)

- write a piece—in any genre—in which the student relates the experience of a being an immigrant. (*Linguistic*)

For more examples of activities with the intelligences infused in them, see the Teaching Methods section which begins on page 84.

Standard: Demonstrates competence in the general skills and strategies of the writing process

The Writing Process

Writing involves a number of processes, each of which builds on the step before it. This page describes steps of the writing process. Subsequent pages provide specific strategies to be implemented at each step.

1. Prewriting

Students need a background of material from which to draw words, thoughts, and ideas before they can write. Prewriting is a brainstorming stage that can be activated through strategies such as semantic webs, word banks, and brainstorming.

2. First-Draft Writing

Determine a purpose and style of writing to give students a direction for their work. Allow students to write freely without undue concern for spelling or grammatical errors at this stage. The focus should be on writing ideas in a logical manner.

3. Response

During this step, the writer is given both verbal and non-verbal feedback on his/her writing from a partner, small group, teacher, or parent. Response provides the writer with information to help him/her clarify ideas and allows for the recognition of strengths in the student's writing.

4. Revision

Writers make their work better through revision by adding detail, using descriptive words or phrases, and possibly changing sentence order for variety or clarification.

5. Editing and Rewriting

In this stage, mechanical errors are corrected. Written works are first edited by the students, alone or in pairs; then rewriting begins. The development of grammar skills can be incorporated within this step.

6. Publishing

Publishing is a way to showcase the author's completed work. Making class books or displaying writing are just two ideas for publishing student work.

Standard: Demonstrates competence in the general skills and strategies of the writing process
Benchmark: Uses prewriting strategies to plan written work

Prewriting Activities

Engaging one or more of the five senses is a sure-fire way to motivate and stimulate pre-writing. Some experiences are listed below:

Sight: Observe a growth process, such as a seed sprouting or an egg hatching.
Make daily observations of the moon, a specific constellation, or cloud formations.
Observe famous paintings, photographs, posters, or magazine pictures.
Read newspapers, food containers, phone books, maps, literature, poems, and dictionaries.
Watch documentaries, historical fiction, or biographies on film and television.
Look at objects under a microscope or through a magnifying glass.

Hearing: Listen to a variety of music, live or recorded.
Hear the songs that the birds sing or the noises of animals in nature.
Listen to books on tape.
Listen for the sounds in a variety of places (home, school, church, ball games, etc.).
Listen to commercials on radio or television.
Listen to the range of voices during the day (from parents to peers to bus drivers to store clerks).

Touch: Feel the pages of various books, magazines, and newspapers.
Touch the petals of a flower, the leaves and bark of a tree, and the spines of a cactus.
Trace the outline of an object: a statue, a picture, a piece of furniture, etc.
Touch things that are hot: a car that's been in the sun, water in a hot shower, etc.
Touch things that are cold: an ice cube, snow, the inside of a freezer, etc.
Feel someone else's skin, hair, and hands.

Smell: Smell freshly picked flowers, newly mown grass, a freshly cut watermelon, or book pages.
Smell the ocean, desert, prairie, or mountain air.
Smell freshly baked bread, cookies, pot roast, fried fish, or other powerful food aromas.
Smell a skunk, dirt, or socks, or smell cabbage or cauliflower as it is cooked.
Smell a campfire, burning leaves, or food cooking on the grill.
Wear a mask for a day and smell the same objects as on the previous day.

Taste: Bite into a lemon, pickle, or apple.
Sample a variety of spices and seasoning by themselves or on various foods.
Taste a food hot; taste the same food when it is cold.
Taste a food in its different forms (e.g., apple: applesauce, apple juice, apple pie, etc.).
Taste an unfamiliar food (e.g., artichoke, jicama, eggplant, couscous, etc.).
Taste different types of water (e.g., tap, bottled, ocean, rain, carbonated, soft, flavored, etc.).

Standard: Demonstrates competence in the general skills and strategies of the writing process
Benchmark: Uses prewriting strategies to plan written work

Sense Matrix

To complete a sense matrix, you must first choose a subject. (This example will use potato chips and ice cubes.) Provide a sample of each object for each child so that the objects can be closely observed and handled. Focusing on one sense at a time, record words and phrases that describe the object. Use the proper spaces on a sense matrix. (See blank one below.) The words and phrases can be incorporated in poems, stories, and descriptive sentences.

Object	Appearance	Feels	Smells	Tastes	Sounds
potato chip	curved, fried, ridged, spoon-like, yellowish	gritty, rough, greasy	tangy, tempting	salty, fried	crunch
ice cube	square, dense, clear, melting	cold, wet, slippery, smooth	fresh, brisk, cool	wet, like cold water	crackle, drip

Students can make their own sense matrix with the outline below. Divide the students into pairs or groups. Let them choose the objects to be described.

Object	Appearance	Feels	Smells	Tastes	Sounds

Standard: Demonstrates competence in the general skills and strategies of the writing process
Benchmark: Uses strategies to draft and revise written work

First-Draft Writing Activities

There are two basic types of writing: the practical and the creative. Practical writing encompasses formal matters of communication, such as invitations, business letters, notes of appreciation, consumer complaint letters, and thank-you notes. Each has a structured format which must be followed, leaving little room for creativity. Creative writing, on the other hand, is a unique and novel expression of self. Words are explored and manipulated, analogies are drawn, comparisons are made, and word pictures are set down on paper.

Further divisions of these two types of writing yield four distinct writing styles or purposes. The chart below describes each and provides sample activities.

Descriptive writing employs details to talk about a given subject.

- Describe someone you admire.
- Tell about a place you go to be alone.
- Describe a video game you like to play.
- Write a poem about your favorite toy.
- Write a description of the classroom.
- Describe someone who bugs you.
- Write a lost and found ad for your dog.

Analytical writing explains how to do something and analyzes people and things.

- Write a commercial for a new product.
- Tell how to make a taco.
- Explain the causes of pollution.
- Write a book review.
- Define the word "friend."
- Tell why you like a particular movie.
- Tell how to solve a math word problem.

Narrative writing tells what happened; feelings are shared.

- Create your own fairy tale.
- Tell about a time you felt lost.
- Tell how you learned to roller skate.
- Tell what it means to be well-liked.
- Write captions for a cartoon.
- Tell about your biggest mistake.
- Tell about a time you were helpful.
- Write a story telling how you failed.

Persuasive writing involves getting others to see and believe in your point of view.

- Write a letter to the editor.
- Tell why people should stop smoking.
- Write an ad for a new product.
- Create a slogan for your class.
- Tell the pros and cons of class rules.
- Create a cartoon strip.
- Tell why something is unfair.

During this first-draft writing phase, attention should focus on writing in a logical manner rather than the mechanics. Spelling and punctuation will be dealt with in the response phase of the process.

Standard: Demonstrates competence in the general skills and strategies of the writing process
Benchmark: Evaluates own and others' writing

Response Activities

The teacher should not be the sole reader of student writing. This responsibility can be shared with partners, small groups, and other adults. Guidelines may be given to the reader so that responses are kept appropriate for this stage of the writing process. (A sample guideline can be found at the bottom of this page.) Conduct whole-class lessons in which everyone can view a writing sample. Guide the students to formulate appropriate response statements.

Student Partners—Pair students to share their writing. (Determine pairs by making two sets of duplicate letters or numeral cards; place them in a paper lunch bag. Students draw a card and find their matching letter or numeral.) Make a class chart to record partners (See diagram at right.) so that the next time this system is employed you can quickly see if students have been paired previously. Any necessary changes can then be made.

	Sue	Ida	Dave	Jeff
Sue				
Ida				
Dave				
Jeff				

Small Groups—Predetermine the purpose of the response group. For example, you may ask the students to choose one part of the writing they did not understand. Within each group, begin making responses for the student who has the least number of letters in his/her entire name. That student reads aloud his/her story, and the other group members take turns responding. Continue having students read and respond in the same manner, going clockwise from the first reader.

Adults—Tell parents and other adults to read their child's writing for its content and ideas, not for the misspelled words or uncapitalized letters. Direct them to write a positive comment on the paper. For example: "Tameka, I enjoyed reading about your roller coaster ride. It made me laugh out loud."

Response Guidelines

Your name: _____

Author's name: _____

1. What I like best about the writing is _____

   _____

2. One thing that needs to be more clear is _____

   _____

3. The author should add more about _____

   _____

Standard: Demonstrates competence in the general skills and strategies of the writing process
Benchmark: Uses strategies to edit and publish written work

Editing Activity

Here is a sample lesson for you to use to instruct students how to vary and change sentence beginnings in a paragraph. Copy the following sentences for all to see.

> *An apple seed is planted in the ground. It is watered. It begins to grow roots. It sprouts. It grows into a tree.*

- Direct students' attention to the sentence beginnings. What do the students notice about them? *(The last four sentences all begin with "It.")*

- Ask the students why they think the beginnings should be more varied. *(To make the story more interesting to read.)*

- Discuss how sentence beginnings can be changed. Establish the following three methods. Rewrite sentences on the board as each method is discussed.

  1. Rearrange Words

  For example, change the third sentence from "It begins to grow roots," to "Roots begin to grow." Make sure that the new sentence conveys the same thought as the original one.

  2. Change Words

  For example, change the word "It" in sentence two to "The seed." Check the rewritten sentence to make sure it conveys the same meaning.

  3. Combine Sentences

  The last two sentences can be combined to read "The seed sprouts and grows into a tree."

  Rewrite the whole paragraph with the new changes.

  > *An apple seed is planted in the ground. The seed is watered. Roots begin to grow. The seed sprouts and grows into a tree.*

- Compare the "before" and "after" paragraphs. Which is more interesting to read? Does the new paragraph say the same thing as the original?

- Discuss any other ways the paragraph can be altered. For example, the first and second sentences could be combined: "An apple seed is planted in the ground and watered."

- Assign small groups to rewrite the following story:

  > *A female moth lays eggs near a food source. A larva hatches from each egg. A larva wraps itself in a cocoon. An adult insect comes out of the cocoon.*

Standard: Demonstrates competence in the general skills and strategies of the writing process
Benchmark: Uses strategies to edit and publish written work

Editing Activity

Editing is the last stage before rewriting a paper for publication. Careful attention is paid here to removing grammatical and spelling errors. Indeed, this is a natural transition for introducing proofreading marks. (See chart below.)

Begin with one or two symbols per lesson, and model with the students a procedure for spotting mistakes. Show them how to focus on one line at a time by covering up the text below with another sheet of paper. Insert the editing symbols and corrections as necessary. Let students work with a partner or small editing group before beginning self-editing.

Proofreading Marks

Editor's Mark	Meaning	Example
_e_	Delete	It was ~~was~~ very tiny.
≡	Capitalize	the boy ran quickly.
/	Use lowercase	Many Athletes ran in the marathon.
∧	Add a word	I want an ice ∧ sundae. (cream)
RO	Run-on sentence	Who's there what do you want? (RO)
frag.	Sentence fragment	Although the peddler's cart. (frag.)
SP	Spelling error	Monkies swung in the trees. (SP)
∪	Reverse letters or words	Five books on were the shelf.
⊙	Add a period	Children played all day⊙
∧ (comma)	Add a comma	I like apples ∧ peaches, and pears.
∨	Add an apostrophe	John's puppy is cute.
∨ ∨	Add quotation marks	Help! I cried.
¶	Begin a new paragraph	"Hello," said Carla. ¶ "Hi," Beth replied.
#	Make a space	I love French # fries.
⌢	Close the space	He lives in the country ⌢ side.
stet	Do not delete (Let it stand.)	The ~~beautiful~~ swan flew away. (stet)

Standard: Demonstrates competence in the general skills and strategies of the writing process
Benchmark: Uses strategies to edit and publish written work

Checklist

This checklist may be used for purposes of self-editing or peer-group editing. Either way, it is best to focus on only one or two areas at a time. The first time through, for example, the writer may check for misspelled words; another time he/she may look for words that need to be capitalized. With groups, you can tell one group to find all the places where commas are needed. Another group can look for words that need to be capitalized. Assign each group a marking pen of a different color—red pens find missing periods, blue pens find missing capitals, etc; or, simply attach a copy of the checklist below to each paper; assign a different direction to each group. Have them check **Yes** or **No** when they have completed their search.

Proofreader's Checklist

Writer's Name: _____

Title of Work: _____

Editor(s): _____

Check **Yes** or **No** after each area you proofread.

1. All sentences begin with a capital letter.	☐ Yes	☐ No
2. All sentences end with the proper punctuation mark.	☐ Yes	☐ No
3. All proper names begin with a capital letter.	☐ Yes	☐ No
4. All words are spelled correctly.	☐ Yes	☐ No
5. There are no missing words.	☐ Yes	☐ No
6. There are no extra words.	☐ Yes	☐ No
7. Commas are used properly.	☐ Yes	☐ No
8. Apostrophes are used properly.	☐ Yes	☐ No
9. Quotation marks are used properly.	☐ Yes	☐ No
10. All words are spaced properly.	☐ Yes	☐ No
11. Paragraphs are used properly.	☐ Yes	☐ No
12. The paper is neat and legible.	☐ Yes	☐ No

Standard: Demonstrates competence in the general skills and strategies of the writing process
Benchmark: Uses strategies to publish written work

Ways to Share Writing

Not all publishable writings have to be put into book form to be shared. Here are some interesting and unusual ways for students to share their writings.

Write it on a paper kite surface. Then fly the kite.

Get your teacher's permission to write it on the chalkboard.

Type it into the computer and e-mail it to a friend.

Have someone videotape you while you read your story.

Make a mobile of your poems.

Write it on an old white shirt or T-shirt and wear it.

Frame it! Buy an inexpensive frame or make your own out of construction paper.

Antique a brown paper bag. Tear the edges, crumple the paper, and paint the edges with brown tempera paint. Let dry before writing on the surface.

Standard: Demonstrates competence in the general skills and strategies of the writing process
Benchmark: Writes an expository composition
Standard: Uses a variety of strategies to identify topics to investigate, uses encyclopedias to gather information for research topics, and compiles information into written reports or summaries
Benchmark: Gathers and uses information for research purposes.

Writing a Report

Follow the steps below to help you plan and write a report.

1. Choose a specific topic. For example, "Sports" covers too many areas, but "Baseball" works because it's a narrower subject.

2. Write five things you want to learn about your topic. For example, five things you might want to learn about baseball might include the following:

    (1) The size of the playing field

    (2) How many players and teams are needed to play

    (3) When and where the first baseball game was played

    (4) What equipment is needed

    (5) Who invented baseball

3. Arrange the five things you wanted to learn in logical order. For example:

    (1) Who invented baseball

    (2) When and where the first baseball game was played

    (3) The size of the playing field

    (4) What equipment is needed

    (5) How many players and teams are needed to play

4. Find out answers to your questions by doing research. Look in encyclopedias, biographies, and textbooks. Also check magazines or newspapers. Write notes on index cards. Include the name and author of the book or magazine you read.

5. Write two or three sentences (or more!) about each of the five things you wanted to learn.

6. Make a bibliography. At the end of your report—on a separate page—write the title and author of all the books in which you found information for your report.

Standard: Demonstrates competence in the general skills and strategies of the writing process
Benchmark: Writes narrative accounts

Writing a Narrative Story

Complete this activity after reading *Mr. Popper's Penguins* by Richard and Florence Atwater (Little Brown, 1988).

A narrative story describes the way in which events happen. An important aspect of a narrative is called point of view. The point of view refers to who is telling the story.

Mr. Popper's Penguins is a narrative because it describes the events caused by the arrival of Captain Cook. It is told in the *third person* (i.e., he, she, it, they) by a narrator—someone who is not involved in the story but is able to see what everyone is doing (and, in some cases, the third person narrator knows what everyone is thinking).

Another type of point of view is called *first person*. In a first-person narrative, a narrator tells the story from personal experience as it is happening (or happened) to him or her. In a first-person narrative, the narrator uses "I" to refer to himself or herself.

Now You Try!: For this section, you will write a short, narrative story. Select a point of view and use it to describe Captain Cook's journey from Antarctica to Stillwater. Before you write your rough draft, it will help to brainstorm.

Point of View: _____

_____

1. What is Captain Cook's mode of transportation? _____

   _____

2. How long does his journey take? _____

   _____

3. How does he feel on the different parts of his journey? _____

   _____

4. Are there any problems on the trip? _____

   _____

Once you have gathered your thoughts, use a separate sheet of paper to write your story.

Standard: Demonstrates competence in the general skills and strategies of the writing process
Benchmarks: Writes in response to literature; writes personal letters

Write a Letter to a Character

Cut out the five rectangles at the bottom of the page. Then paste each one on the dotted line next to the matching part of a letter. (**Note:** The rectangles may need to be posted horizontally or vertically on the page, depending on the direction of the dotted line.) Finally, write a letter to a character from a story.

☐ _ _ _ _ _ _ _ _ _ _ _ _ _ _ _   _____

_____   _ _ _ _ _ _ _ _ _ _ _ _ _ ◯

| | _____

| _____

| _____

| _____

| _____

| _____

| _____

| _____

| _____

☆ _____

△ _ _ _ _ _ _ _ _ _ _ _ _   _____

◇ _ _ _ _ _ _ _ _ _ _   _____

| ◯ **Greeting** | ☐ **Date** | ☆ **Message** |

| △ **Closing** | ◇ **Signature** |

Standard: Demonstrates competence in the general skills and strategies of the writing process
Benchmarks: Writes stories or essays that convey an intended purpose
Writes in response to literature

You Be the Critic

Complete this activity after reading *Mr. Popper's Penguins* by Richard and Florence Atwater (Little Brown, 1988.)

Teacher Note: Collect a variety of reviews (movies, books, etc.) from the newspaper and bring them to class. Then distribute the assignment below.

Before many people see a play, movie, or opera, they read a review in the newspaper to find out if a critic thought it was good. A critic is someone who reviews these events and writes about the good and bad parts for the newspaper or television. Read the reviews your teacher brought into class. Discuss with your classmates whether or not the critic thought the object of the review was any good. How can you tell?

Now, use your imagination to pretend you are a newspaper critic. Your assignment is to review Popper's Performing Penguins.

Here are some things to consider:

1. What did you like about the performance?
2. What didn't you like about the performance?
3. How did you feel during the performance?
4. What suggestions do you have?

Brainstorm your ideas here. Write your review on the back of this sheet or on another piece of paper.

_____

_____

_____

_____

_____

_____

_____

_____

Standard: Demonstrates competence in the general skills and strategies of the writing process
Benchmark: Writes in response to literature

Parallel Poetry

Complete this activity after reading *The Desert Is Theirs* by Byrd Baylor (Aladdin, 1987).

Use the form of poetry in the book to write your own poem. In the left column below, copy the indicated sections with the words arranged just as they are in the book. In the right column, add your own words to make an original parallel poem. Use other parts of the book to write your own parallel poems.

Book Text *The Desert Is Theirs*	**Student Poem** *"The Earth Is Ours"*
This is no place ————————— ————————— ————————— ————————— ————————— ————————— green . . . This is for hawks ————————— ————————— ————————— ————————— ————————— and ————————— ————————— It is for them.	This is no place for anyone who wants bombs and wars and everything red red red . . . This is for people that like only ————————— and————————— that————————— in the ————————— and that choose ————————— It is for US. Continue in the same fashion for other portions of *The Desert Is Theirs*.

Standard: Demonstrates competence in the general skills and strategies of the writing process
Benchmark: Writes in response to literature
Standard: Demonstrates competence in the general skills and strategies for reading a variety of literary texts
Benchmark: Understands simple dialogues and how they relate to a story

"The Old One Died Today."

Complete this activity after reading *Annie and the Old One* by Miska Miles (Little Brown, 1985).

Annie and her mother took the rug they had finished to the trading post. The next day, when they awoke, they discovered that the Old One had died in her sleep.

Activity: Work in groups of three to create the dialogue between Annie and her parents concerning the death of the Old One. On the short lines below, write the name of the character who is speaking; write the characters' names in all capital letters, and place a colon after each (for example, "ANNIE:"). On the longer lines, write what the person is saying. When your group has finished, present your conversation to the class.

Standard: Demonstrates competence in the general skills and strategies of the reading process
Benchmark: Using a glossary, a dictionary, and a thesaurus to determine the meaning of unknown words

Using Your Vocabulary

The object of this exercise is to add at least four practical and useable words to your working vocabulary—instantly!

1. Select a newspaper article that you find interesting. (A passage from a book you are reading will work, too.)

2. Read the article or passage carefully. As you read, write down at least two words that you know but that you do not use in your working vocabulary.

3. Write down two words you either do not know at all or are unsure of.

4. For each word:
   a) Read aloud the sentence that contains the word.
   b) Copy the sentence.
   c) Guess at the meaning of the word. Discuss the word with others, if you can.
   d) Check the meaning of the word in your dictionary.
   e) Use the word in a sentence of your own.

Word #1 _____ Sentence from passage _____

_____

Meaning (your guess)_____
Your own sentence _____

_____

Word #2 _____ Sentence from passage _____

_____

Meaning (your guess)_____
Your own sentence _____

_____

Word #3 _____ Sentence from passage _____

_____

Meaning (your guess)_____
Your own sentence _____

_____

Word #4 _____ Sentence from passage _____

_____

Meaning (your guess)_____
Your own sentence _____

_____

Standard: Demonstrates competence in the general skills and strategies of the reading process
Benchmarks: Previews texts; makes predictions about a text

"I Predict . . ."

Use the following activity to heighten students' pre-reading interest in any story.

Materials:

- copies of illustrations from the book

- copies of various short quotes from the book

Directions:

1. Distribute one copy of either a quoted passage or a picture to each student in your class.

2. Tell the students that you will soon read them a story, but first you want to give them a chance to get to know a little about it. Explain to the students who received pictures that you want them to move around the room telling everyone they meet what they think is happening in the picture. Ask the students with the quotes to read the quotations (with as much expression as possible) to everyone they meet.

3. Have the students circulate around the classroom for about 10 minutes. Encourage them to talk to as many of their classmates as possible.

4. Before you read the story, ask the students if they have any predictions about what happens in the story. Write the predictions on butcher paper or chart paper.

5. After reading the story, refer to the students' predictions. Ask the students if they were surprised by anything in the story.

6. Put the pictures and quotes in sequential order after reading the story, and ask students to retell the story using the passages and illustrations.

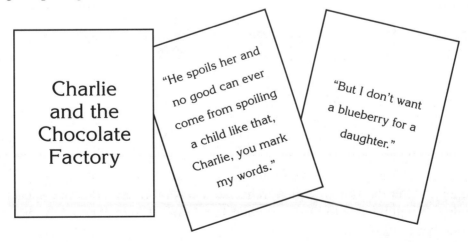

Standard: Demonstrates competence in the general skills and strategies for reading a variety of literary texts
Benchmarks: Applies reading skills and strategies to a variety of literary passages and texts; knows the defining characteristics of a variety of literary forms and genres

Present a Skit

Complete this activity after reading several fables.

Experience the fables you read by presenting a skit illustrating a scene or event from one of them. Work with three or four other students to pick a scene or event you would like to present as a skit. Use the organizer below to help you plan your skit.

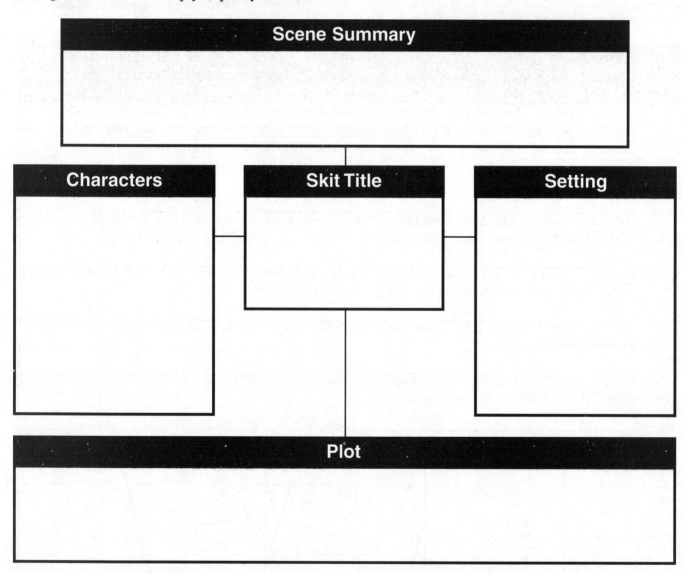

As you work together to write your skit, you may want to include the use of a few special props or some simple scenery. After the skit is written, rehearse it several times. Practice speaking loudly and clearly so the audience will be able to hear and understand you. When everyone in your group feels ready, present your skit to the class.

Standard: Demonstrates competence in the general skills and strategies for reading a variety of literary texts
Benchmarks: Knows defining characteristics of a variety of literary forms and genres; identifies similarities and differences among literary works in terms of setting, characters, and events

A Fairy Tale Recipe

Most fairy tales have many elements in common. These elements are listed below. Create a chart of stories and elements similar to the one shown below, and post it in the classroom. As stories are read, discuss them and fill in the chart. Students should be able to pinpoint which elements apply to each story or character. By learning to synthesize this information, the students should be able to apply these elements in writing their own fairy tales.

Clues	Jack and the Beanstalk	Red Riding Hood	The Three Little Pigs	Hansel and Gretel	The Three Bears	The Talking Eggs
The fairy tale begins, "Once upon a time . . ."						
The fairy tale happens long ago and far away.						
Some characters are royalty.						
Some characters are good; some are evil.						
There is a problem to solve.						
Someone makes a plan to solve the problem.						
There is some magic in the fairy tale.						
Something happens in threes.						
Someone gets a reward.						
There is a "happily ever after" ending.						

Standard: Demonstrates competence in the general skills and strategies for reading a variety of literary texts
Benchmarks: Understands simple dialogues and how they relate to a story
Makes inferences regarding qualities and motives of characters and the consequences of those characters' actions

What Do You Say?

Complete this activity after reading *The Wump World* by Bill Peet (Houghton Mifflin, 1981).

Based on your understanding of the characters and the situations with which they are faced, create the dialogues that might occur in the suggested meetings below.

Dialogue 1

One wump to another wump as they look up from their peaceful grazing to see spaceships descending to their world . . .

Wump 1: _____

Wump 2: _____

Dialogue 2

The World Chief to his people just after he has ordered the sergeant to plant the flag . . .

World Chief: _____

Reaction of his people: _____

Dialogue 3

A baby wump to his mother upon hearing all the frightening noises while they are underground . . .

Baby Wump: _____

Baby Wump's Mother: _____

Dialogue 4

Three top outer spacemen to each other as they are ordered by the World Chief to find a new and better world . . .

Spaceman 1: _____

Spaceman 2: _____

Spaceman 3: _____

Dialogue 5

All wumps in unison as the Pollutians leave their world . . .

Wumps: _____

Standard: Demonstrates competence in the general skills and strategies for reading a variety of literary texts

Benchmark: Makes connections between characters or simple events in a literary work and people or events in his or her own life

Ways of Life

Complete this activity after reading *Annie and the Old One* by Miska Miles (Little Brown, 1985).

Compare and contrast the Navajo ways of life in the areas listed below with those of your own.

The Navajo Way

living conditions: _____

_____

use of land: _____

ways of income: _____

_____

responsibilities of children: _____

_____

hardships: _____

pleasures: _____

thoughts about death: _____

_____

Your Way

living conditions: _____

_____

use of land: _____

ways of income: _____

_____

responsibilities of children: _____

_____

hardships: _____

pleasures: _____

thoughts about death: _____

_____

Standard: Demonstrates competence in the general skills and strategies for the writing process
Benchmark: Writes in response to literature
Standard: Demonstrates competence in the general skills and strategies for reading a variety of literary texts
Benchmark: Knows the defining characteristics of literary forms and genres

Writing Tall Tales

A tall tale is a story based on fact, but told in a highly exaggerated and humorous way. Define exaggeration for your class as something that goes beyond the truth. Read a variety of tall tales to your class. How do they go "beyond the truth?" Have students discuss what makes each a tall tale. List the reasons on a chart entitled "Tall Tale Exaggerations."

Give students an opportunity to write a tall tale. To help them organize their thoughts, first have the students fold their papers into three columns. They should then label the columns "Character," "Setting," and "Exaggeration." Direct them to fill in the columns by using either their own ideas or the information on the class Tall Tale Exaggerations chart. Then, using this new chart they have made, have each of them write a story. Children may draw a picture to illustrate their story.

Some ideas for stories include the following:

- The Day the Rain Fell Up Instead of Down
- My Wild Pet, Tornado Tilly
- A Tornado Drank Up the Wind
- The Day We Had No Weather

Character	Setting	Exaggeration
Marvelous Marty	Deep in a forest	

Standard: Understands the history of a local community and how communities in North America varied long ago
Benchmark: Knows geographical settings, economic activities, food, clothing, homes, crafts, and rituals of Native American societies long ago

About the Tipi

The tipi (tepee) was not just a simple tent. It was a well-constructed home built to stand up to the harsh weather of the Great Plains. It had to be warm in the winter to protect from the cold and snow, and it had to be cool in the summer to keep people comfortable in the scorching heat. It had to be easily moved from place to place so its inhabitants could follow the buffalo herds.

The name tipi comes from two words: *ti* means "to dwell," *pi* means "used for." The tipi was constructed of a frame of wood poles arranged in a cone shape. This was covered by buffalo hides. The cone shape was very sturdy and could stand up to the very strong prairie winds. Also, there were no pockets to catch water, so it could withstand severe rainstorms as well.

The number of poles for a tipi varied. The average number was about 15. These poles were about 20 feet long and weighed 15–20 pounds each.

Pitching a Tipi

Materials:

- straws (about 20)
- cord or string (to tie straws)

Experiment 1: Take 15 straws and tie them together so they stand up in a cone shape. Describe what happens.

_____

_____

Experiment 2: Now take three (or four) straws and tie them together so they stand up in a cone shape. Describe what happens.

_____

_____

Which way was easier? Why do you think this was so? _____

Now you can see why a three- (or four-) pole frame was used by the Plains tribes. Then the other poles were attached. It was not the men of the tribe but the women who were in charge of constructing, transporting, and erecting the tipi. The snugness and comfort of the tipi reflected the woman's ability as a housekeeper. A well-made tipi was a source of great pride to a woman.

Standard: Understands the history of a local community and how communities in North America varied long ago
Benchmark: Understands the challenges and difficulties encountered by people in pioneer farming communities
Standard: Understands the causes and nature of movements of large groups of people into and within the United States, now and long ago
Benchmark: Knows the various movements of large groups of people in the United States

Traveler's Diary

Complete this activity while reading *The Quilt-Block History of Pioneer Days* by Mary Cobb (The Millbrook Press, 1995).

As people traveled across the country, they often kept records of their trips. Sometimes they would write daily and other times just when something noteworthy happened along the trail. The entries did not need to be long, but the best ones were very descriptive. This became a permanent record of the most important trip the settlers were likely ever to take. They were not only moving from one home to another, they were moving to a whole new lifestyle.

As you listen to and read *The Quilt-Block History of Pioneer Days*, imagine you are one of the children embarking on this adventure. After each section of the book is read, write in your own diary. Be sure to include the date. A starting date and sample entry have been provided for you. Keep in mind that the entire trip is likely to take approximately five months.

Write your diary on a separate sheet of paper. Use the same format as the example below.

April 6, 1853

Today, Father told us that we will be selling our farm and moving to a place called Oregon. He said it is very far away. This is so strange! We have to sell almost everything we own so we can buy things we will need for our trip. Father said it would be a hard trip but one worth the trouble. He said gold was just laying on the ground out there waiting to be gathered up! Imagine! There is much to do to get ready for our journey.

Standard: Understands how democratic values came to be and how they have been exemplified by people, events, and symbols
Benchmark: Understands the basic ideas set forth in the U. S. Constitution

The Preamble

Have students llustrate the lines below, using watercolors. Have them work in small groups to complete a single illustration, or give each student his or her own line. The complete illustrations can be assembled into a class preamble book with the strips below cut out and pasted onto the top of each illustrated page.

We the People of the United States,
in order to form a more perfect Union,
establish Justice,
insure domestic Tranquility,
provide for the common Defense,
promote the General Welfare,
and secure the Blessings of Liberty
to Ourselves and our Posterity,
do ordain and establish this Constitution
for the United States of America.

Standard: Understands how democratic values came to be and how they have been exemplified by people, events, and symbols

Benchmarks: Understands how historical figures in the U.S. and in other parts of the world have advanced the rights of individuals and promoted the common good, and understands the character traits that made these historical figures successful; understands the historical events and democratic values commemorated by major national holidays

Martin Luther King, Jr.

Complete the activity on this page and the next one after reading *Martin Luther King Day* by Linda Lowery (Carolrhoda, 1988).

Use these activities related to Martin Luther King, Jr. to develop critical thinking skills and develop an awareness of Martin Luther King, Jr.

Supporting Statements

Sometimes the answer to a question can be found directly on a page of text. Others have to be inferred or "figured out" using supporting statements. With the students, determine which of the following can be supported by the text in *Martin Luther King Day*.

	Can Be Supported	Can't Be Supported
1. Martin Luther King, Jr. was famous.	☐	☐
2. He was a hard worker.	☐	☐
3. Martin liked to read about George Washington.	☐	☐
4. He was proud that he was black.	☐	☐
5. Everyone liked Martin Luther King's ideas.	☐	☐

Character Traits

Model with the students the following process. Identify a character trait of Martin Luther King, Jr. For example, he was persistent. Ask the students to find evidence of this fact within the text of *Martin Luther King Day*. As a class, brainstorm some of Martin Luther King's character traits and record them on the chalkboard, chart paper, or overhead projector. Direct the students to complete the sentences below.

Martin Luther King, Jr. was_____

I know this because _____

_____

_____

(**Note:** Some possible traits include responsible, proud, fair, strong, studious, peaceful, etc.)

Martin Luther King, Jr. *(cont.)*

Martin Luther King, Jr. had a dream that some day all people, regardless of their color, would be able to live together in peace. Tell about your dream for peace. Draw a picture to go with your story.

I Have a Dream. . . .

Standard: Understands the causes and nature of movements of large groups of people into and within the United States, now and long ago
Benchmarks: Knows the various movements of large groups of people in the history of the U.S.; knows the reasons why various groups migrated to different parts of the U.S.

Songs of the Gold Rush

Every period of history has its special songs. Stephen Foster, America's most famous songwriter of the nineteenth century, wrote many of his compositions around the time of the California Gold Rush. Two of his most famous melodies are "Oh, Susanna" (1848) and "Camptown Races" (1850).

(based on the tune of **"Oh, Susanna"**)
I come from dear old Boston with a washbowl on my knee,
I'm going to California the gold dust for to see.
It rained all night the day I left, the weather it was dry,
The sun so hot I froze to death, dear brother, don't you cry.
Chorus: Oh, Cal-I-for-ny

O-That's the land for me!

I'm going to Sacramento

With a washbowl on my knee.
I jumped aboard the largest ship and traveled on the sea,
And every time I thought of home, I wished it wasn't me!
The vessel reared like any horse that had oats a wealth,
I found it wouldn't throw me, so I thought I'd throw myself! *(CHORUS)*
I thought of all the pleasant times we've had together here,
An' I thought I ought to cry a bit, but I couldn't find a tear,
The pilot's bread was in my mouth, the gold dust in my eye,
And I thought I'm going far away, dear brother, don't you cry. *(CHORUS)*
I soon shall be in 'Frisco and there I'll look around,
And when I see the gold lumps there, I'll pick them off the ground.
I'll scrape the mountains clean, my boys, I'll drain the rivers dry,
A pocketful of rocks bring home, so brother, don't you cry.

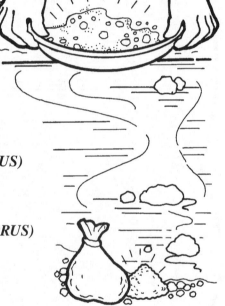

(based on the tune of **"Camptown Races"**)

A bully ship and a bully crew
    Dooda, dooda,
A bully mate and a captain too,
    Dooda, dooda, day.
Then blew ye winds hi-oh
For Cal-i-for-ny-o,
There's plenty of gold so I've been told
On the banks of the Sacramento.
Oh, around the Cape Horn we're bound to go,
    Dooda, dooda,
Around Cape Horn through the sleet and snow,
    Dooda, dooda, day.
Oh, around Cape Horn in the month of May
    Dooda, dooda,

Oh, around Cape Horn is a very long way,
    Dooda, dooda, day.
Ninety days to 'Frisco Bay,
    Dooda, dooda,
Ninety day is darn good pay,
    Dooda, dooda, day.
I wish to God I'd never been born,
    Dooda, dooda,
To go a-sailin' round Cape Horn,
    Dooda, dooda, day.
To the Sacramento we're bound away,
    Dooda, dooda.
To the Sacramento's a heck of a way,
    Dooda, dooda, day.

32

Standard: Understands the causes and nature of movements of large groups of people into and within the United States, now and long ago
Benchmark: Understands the experience of immigrant groups

Ellis Island

Ellis Island was an immigrant processing center that was open from 1892 until 1952. During that time, over 12 million immigrants entered the United States through Ellis Island. Today, more than four out of ten American people can trace their roots to an ancestor who entered America through Ellis Island. Built to process 5,000 new immigrants each day, it often processed twice that number.

Once the immigrants stepped off their boats, large, numbered tags were tied to their clothing. They were taken to the registry hall where, after waiting in long lines, they were examined by doctors. Chalk marks were put on their clothing if any medical problems were suspected. Anyone whose clothing was marked was detained for further examination. About one out of every six people was delayed for as long as four days because of medical problems, and one out of every ten of those delayed was sent back to his/her homeland because the problems were judged to be serious. Those who made it past the medical examination were then questioned by a government inspector. If any answer was suspect, the person would face a board of special inquiry who would decide if the person could stay. If all tests were passed, the average stay on Ellis Island was about five hours.

Simulation

Have students re-enact the arrival of a group of immigrants to Ellis Island. All of the students will be immigrants, except for nine who will play the roles mentioned below.

Have one student hand out tags with numbers to be taped to the immigrants' clothing. One student will act as the medical examiner. He or she will look in the immigrants' eyes, ears, and mouths. The medical examiner may choose about one out of every five immigrants to see the specialist. The person acting as the medical specialist will determine whether the person should be sent back or allowed to remain. The immigrants who pass the medical examination will then be sent to the government inspector. This person will choose to ask each immigrant some of the following questions:

- What is your name?
- How old are you?
- Are you married?
- What is your occupation?
- Can you read or write?
- Where are you from?
- Where are you going in the United States?

- How much money do you have with you?
- Do you have any relatives in the U.S.? If so, do you know their addresses?
- Have you ever been to the United States before? When and where?
- Have you ever been in prison?
- How is your health?

Any immigrant who seems unsure of an answer will be sent to a special inquiry board made up of five students, who will continue to ask questions. This board will then vote to determine whether the person will be allowed to remain in the United States. Follow the simulation with a discussion.

Social Studies

Standard: Understands the causes and nature of movements of large groups of people into and within the United States, now and long ago
Benchmark: Knows the various movements of large groups of people in the history of the U.S.

Who? When? Why?

In *Molly's Pilgrim* by Barabara Cohen (Demco Media, 1993), Molly's family flees a little town in Russia called Goraduk because the Cossacks (Russian soldiers) were persecuting the Jews. When Molly cries to return to her old homeland, Mama comments, "If the Cossacks haven't burned it down."

Throughout history, some groups of people have been treated badly because of their beliefs or principles. Often they have had to leave their homelands in order to survive.

Persecution is only one reason people emigrate. Other reasons include famine, lack of economic opportunities, and the desire for a better education.

What other groups have immigrated to America? Why did they come? In what years did they arrive? How many people came from each country? To find the answers to these questions, do some research. Use encyclopedias and reference books. Use the information you find to fill out the chart below.

Who?	When?	How Many?	Why?
Eastern-European Jews	1880s–1920	about 2½ million	religious persecution

Standard: Understands selected attributes and historical developments of societies in Africa, the Americas, Asia, and Europe
Benchmark: Understands how historians learn about the past if there are no written records

Artifact Inquiry

Topic

Archaeology plays a major role in helping us to understand history.

Objective

Working in groups, students will identify the functions of previously unknown objects by their appearances and/or structures.

Materials

The teacher should bring in one unusual object for each learning team in his or her class. Likely sources for items that students won't be able to easily identify include the following:

- basements

- attics

- antique store

- garage sales

- flea markets

Directions

1. Divide the class into cooperative learning teams, and give each team an object or "artifact" that has been brought to class.

2. Allow each team to examine each object for about three or four minutes. For example, if you have six learning teams, each team should spend three to four minutes inspecting each of the six items before passing each item on to the next team. After several minutes of examination, teams need to rotate objects in a teacher-directed order so that each team will eventually inspect all items available.

3. Brainstorming is an excellent way for team members to share their ideas on the function of the "artifacts." Ask team members to brainstorm by writing suggestions of possible functions for each of the items. While giving an exact identity of the objects may be difficult or even impossible, members of each team can use the final minutes of inspection of each "artifact" to delineate some function of that item. Like an archaeologist separated by time from the owner of a relic, the students need to search for clues as to how each object was used.

Artifact Inquiry *(cont.)*

Directions *(cont.)*

4. Once all teams have examined all objects, teams can be paired to share their information and ideas. The teacher will then reveal each item's actual name and use(s) to the class. Just as archaeologists put their heads together, groups collectively sharing could very well uncover pertinent ideas not noticed by each individual team before. If students give the approximate function(s) of an object, that alone should count as a success.

* **Note to the teacher:** In a five-minute perusal of a basement workshop, a teacher might have discovered an antique glass furniture coaster, a rubber cap for a kitchen chair leg, a brass-plated ornamental eagle for a lamp post, the cleaning implement for a ramrod to a muzzle-loading rifle, and a metal window jamb pulley for a very old double-hung window. It is highly unlikely that more than one or two (if any) of these objects would ever be correctly placed by the students. However, if they said the eagle was "screwed on to something for a decoration," that would be correct due to its threaded bottom. The idea that something was protected by the rubber cap (a kitchen chair leg) would also be acceptable. Students need not be exact, only close in appropriate function.

Background

When archaeologists dig up artifacts, many times they are unearthing certain objects for the first time and must guess the function based on appearance. Further digs in similar locales may shed more light on these objects and give greater credence to a researcher's proposed identification. "Artifact Inquiry," while not having the benefit of further explorations, is similar in a way to the process involved in archaeology. It is an excellent activity for beginning the year in history since archaeology is a fundamental source of our information on many past events and cultures.

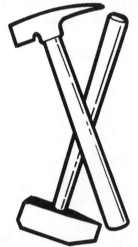

Follow-Up

For those with a real desire to simulate an archaeological dig, bury several related objects in each of several sturdy boxes (again, one box per team). Have students set up a coordinated grid on their box "sites," using string or yarn and tacks to hold the string to the sides of the box. They should then use spoons and old sieves to carefully remove dirt and to detail the location of each find. Old pottery broken into several dull-edged pieces may serve very well as the potential relic. Students could attempt to put the pottery back together again.

Standard: Understands selected attributes and historical developments of societies in Africa, the Americas, Asia, and Europe
Benchmark: Knows significant historical achievements of various cultures of the world

Ancient Wonders

Use an encyclopedia or other reference book to help you fill in the missing information about these magnificent ancient structures.

Name	Location	When Built	Description
			tombs built for Egyptian kings
	Babylon	between 605 and 562 B.C.	
			huge bronze statue of the god Apollo
Temple of Artemis		about 550 B.C.	
Lighthouse of Alexandria		between 283–246 B.C.	
	Olympia, Greece		gold and ivory statue of Zeus
	Halicarnassus		huge white marble tomb

Standard: Understands selected attributes and historical developments of societies in Africa, the Americas, Asia, and Europe
Benchmark: Knows the significant scientific and technological achievements of various historical societies

Make a Sumerian Invention Wheel

After completing the study of Sumerian culture, have students make a wheel that shows many of the inventions and achievements of the Sumerians.

Materials

1. Provide students with the invention wheel patterns (pages 39–40), large sheets of colored construction paper, white writing paper, scissors, glue, brads, and drawing materials.

2. Gather resource books that describe the achievements of the Sumerians.

Directions

1. Distribute the materials to each student. Tell them that they will each create a visual aid to show some of the achievements and inventions of the Ancient Sumerians. Since the Sumerians are considered to be the first to use wheeled vehicles, it is fitting that the visual aid is in the shape of a Sumerian wheel.

2. Discuss the categories that students will research and divide the class into small research groups. Have them organize the information and label it.

    Transportation—the invention of sailboats and wheeled vehicles

    Irrigation—the invention of irrigation systems to bring water to barren ground

    Use of Clay—pottery, houses, bricks, pottery wheel, etc.

    Use of Copper and Bronze—plows, weapons, jewelry, etc.

    Writing System—the invention of cuneiform writing

    Numbers and Measurement—the use of a number system based on 60, the calendar, time, units of measurement, etc.

    Written Law—rules by which people were to live

    Religious Tradition—how the Sumerians worshipped

3. Tell each student to write the information on a piece of paper labeled "Sumerian Inventions and Achievements." Have each student glue his or her paper on one side of a piece of construction paper.

4. Have students use the invention pie chart pattern to draw and color pictures of each category. Have them cut out the pattern and glue it next to the invention list on the construction paper.

5. Have students color and cut out the Sumerian wheel pattern. Show students how to attach the invention wheel to the construction paper with a brad so the wheel can turn to highlight the categories one at a time.

6. Have students share their wheels and research with the class.

Make a Sumerian Invention Wheel *(cont.)*

Make a Sumerian Invention Wheel *(cont.)*

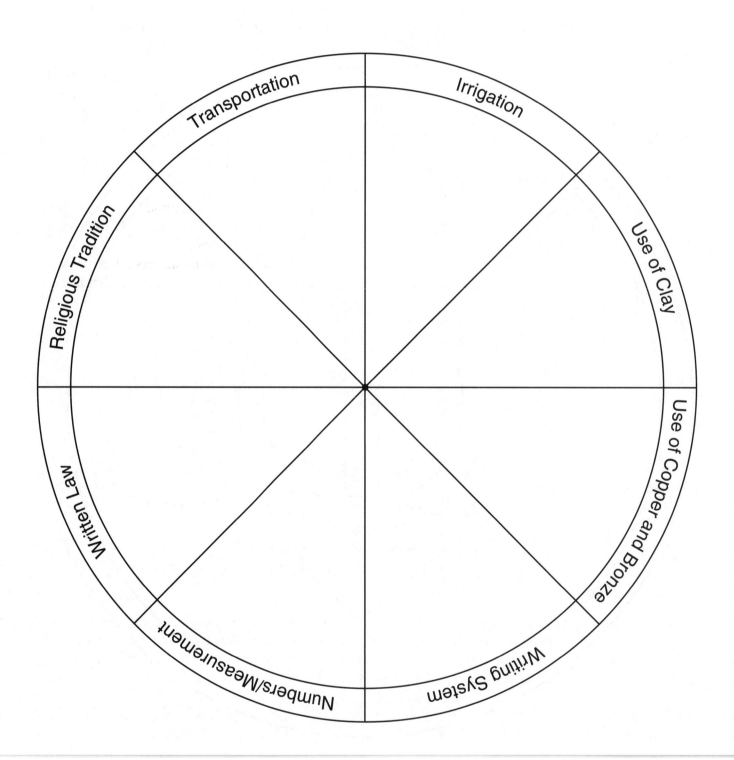

Standard: Understands and applies basic and advanced properties of the concepts of numbers

Benchmark: Understands the basic difference between odd and even numbers

Math Magic with Money

Try fooling your friends who are good at mathematics. You can do this several times before they catch on. To solve the magic, they will have to think mathematically.

Odd or Even

Here is a trick. This depends on straight arithmetic. It works because most people look for a trick rather than thinking about the experiment. This one can even be done over a telephone.

Give your friend a penny and a dime. Ask him or her to hold the penny in one hand and the dime in the other. Then have him or her do a little simple arithmetic for you. Have him or her multiply the value of the coin in his or her right hand by 2, 4, or 6 and memorize the answer. Then have him or her multiply the value of the coin in his left hand by 3, 5, or 7. (In both cases, he or she has a free choice of which number to use as the multiplier.) Then ask him or her to add the two answers together and give you the total. You can then tell him or her which hand each of the coins is in.

Why It Works: When we think of coins, we think of pennies and dimes, not numbers. A dime is an even number, 10, while the penny is an odd number, 1. It is because one value is even, while the other is odd, that the trick works.

You will notice that you first ask that the coin in the right hand be multiplied by an even number. If the coin is the even one (the dime) the product will be even. If it is the odd coin (the penny), the product will also be even.)

Then you multiply the left hand by an odd number. That way, if the hand has the dime, the product will be even, but if it has the penny, the product will be odd. It is the product of this hand that gives you the clue. When the products are added together, the total will be odd only if the left-hand product is odd, and that will happen only if the left hand holds the penny!

Because of this difference, all you have to know is whether the answer your friend gives you is even or odd. If odd, the penny is in the left hand; if even, the dime is in the left hand.

Standard: Uses basic and advanced procedures while performing the processes of computation

Benchmark: Adds, subtracts, multiplies, and divides whole numbers and decimals

How Much Do You Weigh?

How much do you weigh? Your weight depends upon where you are. If you were to visit other planets and moons with more or less mass than Earth's, a scale would show that you weigh a different amount than you do on Earth. Complete the chart to find out how much you would weigh on the planets in our solar system and on the moon. (**Note:** Surface gravities listed here are calculated in relation to Earth's.)

Planet	Surface Gravity		Your Weight on Earth	New Weight
Mercury	.38	x		
Venus	.90	x		
Earth	1.00	x		
Mars	.38	x		
Jupiter	2.64	x		
Saturn	1.13	x		
Uranus	.89	x		
Neptune	1.13	x		
Pluto	.06	x		
Earth's Moon	.17	x		

42

How Much Do You Weigh? *(cont.)*

Make a bar graph to show the results of your calculations from your activity sheet (page 42).

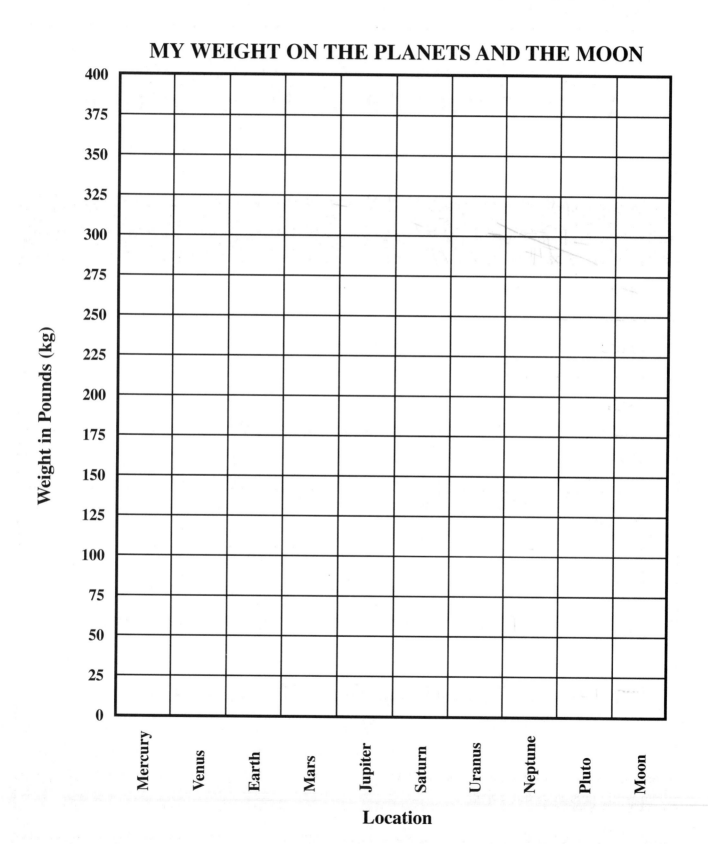

Standard: Uses basic and advanced procedures while performing the processes of computation
Benchmark: Determines the effects of addition, subtraction, multiplication, and division on the size and order of a number

The Importance of Math Symbols

First used in 1537, the equal sign (=), the plus sign (+), and minus sign (-) advanced the development of mathematics.

Try the problems below. They are missing the symbols for the four operations—addition (+), subtraction (-), multiplication (x), and division (÷). Work from left to right. Add the operation symbols between each pair of numbers so that the given answer can be reached.

a. 5 _____ 6 _____ 1 _____ 3 _____ 4 = 9

b. 7 _____ 3 _____ 4 _____ 10 _____ 2 = 70

c. 14 _____ 7 _____ 63 _____ 3 _____ 3 _____ 9 = 10

d. 59 _____ 2 _____ 2 _____ 9 _____ 3 = 10

e. 42 _____ 4 _____ 2 _____ 16 _____ 10 = 10

f. 110 _____ 12 _____ 10 _____ 14 _____ 12 _____ 10 _____ 12 = 12

g. 13 _____ 7 _____ 19 _____ 60 _____ 20 _____ 10 = 15

Challenge: Try writing some problems of your own leaving out the operation signs. Exchange them with classmates and solve.

Standard: Uses basic and advanced procedures while performing the processes of computation

Benchmark: Solves real world problems involving number operations

Shopping Spree

With two classmates, imagine that you are going shopping at a store in your city to purchase school supplies. You and your classmates have $45.00 to spend at the store. Create a detailed list, showing how you and your classmates would spend the money. The chart below shows the items available for purchase and their prices. Your goal is to try to spend as close to $45.00 as possible without going over. There is no limit on amounts purchased; however, at least five different items must be purchased by each classmate.

School Supplies Price List
5 ballpoint pens . . . .$.89
12 pencils . . . .$.79
50 index cards $1.29
80-page spiral notebook $1.19
marker set $2.99
3-ring binder $3.29
colored-pencil pack $1.39
scissors $2.19
2 pocket folders . . . .$.29
10 high-density disks $6.99

Write your detailed list in the table below. Continue on the back of this paper, if necessary.

Consumer	Item	Quantity	Cost

Standard: Uses basic and advanced procedures while performing the processes of computation
Benchmark: Adds, subtracts, multiplies, and divides whole numbers and decimals

Monkeys' Lunch

Use the monkey manipulatives on page 47 to help solve these problems.

1. If the bananas were divided equally among 4 monkeys, how many bananas would each monkey get?

   Example:

   | 28 ÷ 4= | | 7 |

2. If the coconuts were divided equally among 2 monkeys, how many coconuts would each monkey get?

3. If the pineapples were divided equally among 2 monkeys, how many pineapples would each monkey get?

4. If the candy bars were divided equally among 5 monkeys, how many candy bars would each monkey get?

5. If all of the food was divided equally among 15 monkeys, how many pieces of food would each monkey get?

6. If the coconuts and bananas were divided equally among 7 monkeys, how many coconuts and bananas would each monkey get?

   (coconuts)

   (bananas)

Monkey Manipulatives

This sheet has enough manipulatives for one student, pair, or group to use for page 46. Allow students to color and cut out their sets of manipulatives. Laminate the manipulatives if you wish to use them again in the future.

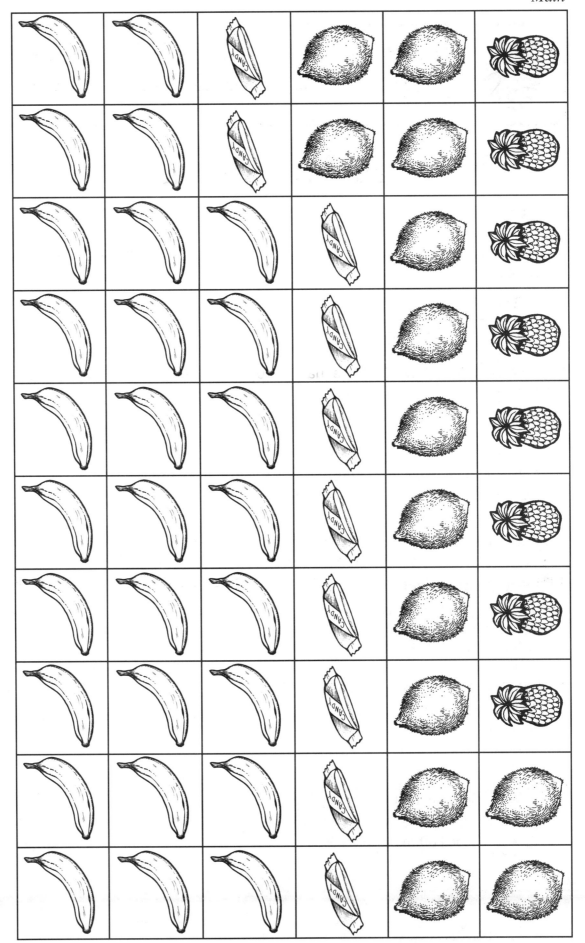

Standard: Uses basic and advanced procedures while performing the processes of computation
Benchmark: Performs basic mental computations

Making Math in Your Head

Doing math in your head means learning how to simplify. There are a number of ways to do this. You can . . .

- reorder numbers.
- break up numbers.
- use equivalents.
- round off and approximate.

1. Reordering Numbers

a. You are in the grocery store and you want to figure out quickly whether you have enough money to buy three items. You need to know how much 14, 38, and 6 are when totaled. Do the following: Reorder the numbers first into (14 + 6) + 38. Fourteen plus six is easy: it is 20. Now add 38 to 20, which is also easy: 20 + 38 = 58.

b. You want to multiply 25 x 33 x 8. First, multiply 25 x 8. That is simple! It is 200. Then multiply 200 x 33 by multiplying 33 x 2 (Answer: 66) and then 66 x 100 (Answer: 6600).

c. You need to multiply a fraction by a whole number (for example, ¾ x 48). First, divide 48 by 4. The answer is 12. Then multiply 12 by 3. The answer is 36.

2. Breaking Up Numbers

You want to multiply 12 x 19. First, break the numbers up into multiples of 10, so you now have (10 + 2) x 19, which is (10 x 19) + (2 x 19), and that in turn is 190 + 38. The answer is 228.

3. Using Equivalents

Fractions can be very useful numbers. For example, if you want to multiply 50 by any number, simply multiply the number by 100 and then divide it by 2. 50 is half of 100. Remember that ¼ is the same as .25; therefore, ⅛ is one half of ¼ or .125, and ⅓ is .333 , ⅔ is .67, and so forth. Using these may not give you an exact answer, but it can give you one which is approximate.

4. Round Off and Approximate

To round off a number, drop the unwanted digits on the right. If the first digit dropped is 5 or greater, increase the preceding digit by 1. If the first digit dropped is less than 5, leave the preceding digit unchanged. For example:

- ⅓ rounded off to three places is .333
- ⅓ rounded off to two places is .33
- ⅓ rounded off to one place is .3
- ⅔ rounded off to three places is .667
- ⅔ rounded off to two places is .67
- ⅔ rounded of to one place is .7

Making Math in Your Head *(cont.)*

Try doing the following problems in your head.

1. **Additions**

   a. $23 + $64 = _____

   b. $34 + $159 = _____

   c. $18 + $139 = _____

   d. $57 + $166 = _____

2. **Subtractions**

   a. You paid $64 for a coat, and your friend paid $47. How much more did you pay?

   _____

   b. You paid $83 for insurance, and your friend paid $69. How much more did you pay?

   _____

   c. You paid $221 for rent, and your friend paid $176. How much more did you pay?

   _____

3. **Making Change**

   a. You bought items for a total of $3.80 and handed the clerk $5. How much change did you get?

   _____

   b. You paid $16.25 for a shirt and handed the clerk $20.00. How much change did you get?

   _____

   c. You bought canned goods for $3.54 and produce for $4.89. What is your total change from $10.00?

   _____

4. **Approximating**

   a. You want to buy items costing $11.98, $15.95, and $7.96. How much are they all together?

   _____

   b. You want to buy items costing $3.99, $24.88, and $5.95. How much are they all together?

   _____

   c. You want to buy items costing $8.88, $56.75, and $12.90. How much are they all together?

   _____

   d. A pair of shoes that is regularly $44.99, is on sale for $26. How much will you save?

   _____

   e. A jacket that is regularly $69, is on sale for $44.95. How much will you save?

   _____

   f. A shirt that is regularly $22 is on sale for $17.99. How much will you save?

   _____

Bonus: Now go into small groups and make up some problems from each category for one another to solve.

Standard: Understands and applies basic and advanced properties of the concepts of measurement
Benchmark: Understands basic measures—perimeter, area, volume, capacity, mass, angle, and circumference

Sandy Measurement

Students will love working with sand in this activity in which they explore the relationship between standard and non-standard units of measurement.

Materials

- large trays
- sand
- scoops (coffee, detergent, etc.)
- 8-oz. (850 mL) cups or milk containers
- pint-sized (500 mL) milk containers
- quart-sized (1L) milk containers
- gallon-sized (4L) milk container
- permanent marker

Teacher Preparation

1. Cut the tops off the milk cartons so students can scoop and pour sand in and out of the containers easily. (You may wish to ask parents to send in containers.)

2. Mark each container according to its unit of measure.

3. Have students seated in groups of five to six children. Each group should have one large tray filled with sand and at least one of each of the following: scoop, cup, pint, quart, or gallon containers. This activity may also be done as a learning center. Rotate students through the center allowing enough time for experimentation and completion of the activity page.

Directions

1. Give each group a time of exploration with the materials. After 10 minutes or so, ask the students if they noticed anything about the various scoops and containers. Brainstorm and list these on the board.

2. Talk about standard units of measure. Have the children experiment and see if they notice any relationship between the measuring tools (e.g., if a certain amount of one measuring tool equals another). After a few minutes, list their responses.

3. Pass out the Sandy Measurement handout on page 51. Have groups work together to explore answers.

Extension: Have students bring in various other scoops and measuring tools. Set up a tray or a small, inflatable child's pool filled with sand as a center in the room. Children can explore relationships between standard and non-standard measurements on their own.

Sandy Measurement *(cont.)*

Work with your group to find the answers below.

A. 2 cups equal _____ pint.

B. 4 cups equal _____ quart.

C. 2 pints equal _____

D. 4 quarts equal _____

E. 8 cups equal _____

F. 6 cups equal _____ or _____ quart(s) and _____ pint.

G. 1 quart equals_____ pints or_____cups.

H. 1 gallon equals_____pints or_____quarts or_____cups.

Bonus:

A. How many cups in 1 gallon + 1 quart + 1 pint? _____

B. How many pints in 3 gallons? _____

C. How many quarts in two gallons? _____

Standard: Understands and applies basic and advanced properties of the concepts of measurement

Benchmarks: Understands basic measures—perimeter, area, volume, capacity, mass, angle, and circumference; understands the relationship between measures

Perimeter Versus Area

This math activity requires students to investigate the relationship between perimeter and area. Students may work alone or in a cooperative group.

Materials

- tape
- string
- scissors
- straight pins
- thick cardboard
- pencils and markers
- one-inch (2.54 cm) tiles, 70 or more per group
- "Perimeter Versus Area" activity (page 53), one for each student
- graph paper with smaller squares, several sheets for each student
- graph paper with one-inch squares (2.54 cm), several sheets for each student

Directions

Ask students to go directly to their cooperative groups and follow the directions on the activity page to explore the relationship between perimeter and area. Encourage students to discuss the process and to compare their diagrams and solutions.

When everyone has completed Perimeter Versus Area, meet back in the large group to discuss and compare answers.

To Simplify: Have an aide, older student, or parent volunteer work through the activity with the students, helping them to discuss and clarify their ideas.

To Expand: Have students explore the relationship between perimeter and area, using shapes other than squares and rectangles.

Processing: Allow time for the students to discuss the activity. Was the activity easy or difficult? Was there anything about it that surprised you? What? Explain.

Perimeter Versus Area *(cont.)*

Student _____

Group _____

1. Cut a piece of string 16 inches (40.6 cm) long. Put the ends together with tape without overlapping the ends of the string.

2. Lay a piece of graph paper with 1-inch (2.5 cm) squares on top of the heavy cardboard.

3. Lay the piece of string on the graph paper so that it forms a square with 4-inch (10.2 cm) sides. Use pins to hold the corners. Draw around the square you just made.

4. You already know the perimeter of the squares because you cut the string to be 16 inches (40.6 cm) long. What is the area of the square? (Count the squares inside the string on the graph paper and write the number.)

5. Now, move the string to another area of the graph paper. Lay the string so it forms a rectangle 7 inches (17.8 cm) long and 1 inch (2.5 cm) wide. Use pins to hold the corners, and draw around the rectangle you just made.

6. You already know the perimeter of the rectangle because you are still using the string that you cut to be 16 inches (40.6 cm) long. What is the area of the rectangle? (Count the squares inside the string on the graph paper and write the number.)

   What is the area? _____

7. Do this whole experiment over again, making a rectangle that is 6 inches (15.2 cm) long and 2 inches (5.1 cm) wide.

   What is the area? _____

8. Try the experiment with strings of different lengths.

9. Talk and write about the results in your group. What conclusions can you draw?

   _____

   _____

   _____

   _____

   _____

Standard: Understands and applies basic and advanced concepts of statistics and data analysis
Benchmark: Organizes and displays data in simple bar graphs

A Taste for TV: Graph It!

Find out about your classmates' TV viewing habits by doing the following activity.

1. Pretend your principal has asked you to give him or her a report about how much TV and what kinds of shows kids are watching. He or she thinks kids are watching too much TV. Do you agree? Gather data to confirm or disprove his or her hypothesis. You will need a pencil, ruler, colored pencils, and the completed tally sheet below.

2. Survey your class and others in the school by asking them to select the three categories of TV that they watch most frequently. Next, ask them how much time they spend in one week watching TV. Use tally marks on the charts.

3. Make two bar graphs of the results on the back of this page. Title graph one "Our TV Choices" and graph two "Time Spent Watching TV." Label the left scale "Students" on both graphs and use increments of two students for each line. On graph one, write in the TV choices along the bottom scale. On graph two, write in the TV-watching times along the bottom. Keep your words neat and evenly spaced.

4. Use your ruler to make vertical bars of the results from the tally sheet. Next, color each bar a different color.

5. Discuss your findings as a class.

Tally Chart

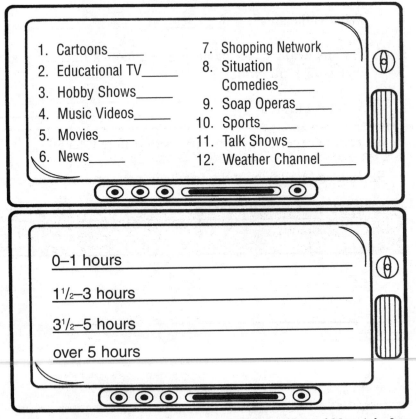

TV Shows

1. Cartoons_____
2. Educational TV_____
3. Hobby Shows_____
4. Music Videos_____
5. Movies_____
6. News_____
7. Shopping Network_____
8. Situation Comedies_____
9. Soap Operas_____
10. Sports_____
11. Talk Shows_____
12. Weather Channel_____

TV Time

0–1 hours
1½–3 hours
3½–5 hours
over 5 hours

54

Standard: Understands and applies basic and advanced concepts of probability
Benchmark: Understands that the word *chance* refers to the likelihood of an event occurring

Flip of a Coin

If you flip a coin with a friend to decide who will be the next captain of your soccer game, you are involved in a study of probability. What are your odds if you choose heads? There are two sides of a coin. You have chosen one side, so your chances are one in two, or 50/50.

Try the experiments below to identify possible outcomes and determine whether or not they are equally likely.

A knowledge of probability will give you an advantage over your friends. Do the following experiments to investigate your chances.

Experiment #1—Tossing a Coin

Chart the results on the chalkboard.

Toss the penny.	Outcomes	Chances	Probability
	heads tails	There is 1 chance out of 2 of getting heads.	The probability of getting heads is 1/2.

Experiment #2—Random Coin Choosing

Draw out one coin without looking.

Bag with 5 pennies, 5 dimes, 5 nickels	Outcomes	Chances	Probability
		There is 1 chance out of 3 of getting a dime.	The probability of getting a dime is 1/3.

Standard: Understands basic features of the Earth
Benchmark: Knows the major difference between fresh and ocean waters

Water, Water Everywhere

Science Concepts

- Much of Earth is covered by water.
- Much of the water has salt.
- This salty water is the oceans and seas.

Question

How does the ocean get its salt?

Discovery Experience

Gather your students together and tell them they are going to be learning about how the ocean gets its salt.

Materials

- 2 paper cups (per child)
- coffee filter
- table salt
- 1 sheet of black construction paper
- modeling clay
- glue or paste
- dirt
- measuring spoon, tablespoon
- ceramic or plastic dish
- ice pick (for teacher's use only)

Directions

1. Using an ice pick, poke several holes in the bottom of several paper cups. Give one to each child.
2. Ask the children to put the coffee filter inside the paper cup with holes.
3. Ask each child to put a tablespoon (15 g) of dirt and a tablespoon (15 g) of salt into their second paper cups and mix these two ingredients together.
4. Tell the students to pour this dirt and salt into the paper cup with the coffee filter.
5. Tell the students to put a sheet of black construction paper on the dish.
6. Ask the children to make three small balls of modeling clay. Then, ask them to prop up the cup with the dirt mixture above the black paper, using the clay balls as little legs.
7. Tell the students to put three tablespoons (45 mL) of water in the cup and allow it to drain out onto the paper.
8. Have the children place their black pieces of paper in a place where they can dry out, and then observe what is on the paper. Explain to them that the white crystals they see are the salt.

What Scientists Know

—The dirt on Earth contains salt, and when it rains, the rainwater dissolves salt from the soil.

—This salt finds its way to rivers that flow into the oceans, filling the ocean with salt.

—Over 70 percent of Earth's surface is covered by water.

—The average depth of the ocean is 12,500 feet (3,791 m), almost 2 ½ miles (4 km).

—Ninety percent of the ocean is more than 650 feet (197 m) deep.

Standard: Understands basic features of the Earth
Benchmark: Knows that clouds are made of tiny droplets of water

Make a Cloud

Science Concept

- A cloud is a collection of tiny water droplets or ice bits hanging in the air.

Question

What is a cloud?

Discovery Experience

Ask the children if they have ever made a cloud. On a very cold day, the moisture from your warm breath condenses as it is cooled by contact with the air. If you have ever "seen your breath" on a very cold day, you have made a cloud! Try this activity that illustrates the same concept.

Materials

- two clear plastic cups
- ¼ cup (64 mL) of hot water
- flashlight (optional)
- magnifying glass (optional)

Directions

1. Pour ¼ cup (64 mL) hot water into one plastic cup.
2. Flip the second cup upside down and place it over the first cup. Make sure the rims meet to prevent the "cloud" from escaping.
3. Look into the cup, and you will see a cloud. Dim the lights and shine a flashlight into the cup for an even better look. What is a cloud? From where did the cloud or water droplets you see inside the cups come? The heat in the water makes the water evaporate into the air and become a gas called water vapor. The water vapor moved upward and turned from a gas back into a liquid when it encountered the cooler air in the top cup.
4. Draw a picture of what is observed inside the cup.

What Scientists Know

—Clouds are made up of billions of tiny ice or water droplets that have condensed around specks of dust or salt.

—Water vapor changes from a gas to a liquid, and clouds form when warm and cold air meet.

—Cool air cannot hold as much water vapor (water in its gaseous form) as warm air, so some of the water vapor condenses or turns into tiny water droplets.

—When these tiny drops of liquid collect together, they form a cloud.

—A cloud formed in the cup when the warm, moisture-saturated air in the bottom cup moved upward and met the cooler air in the top cup.

Standard: Understands basic Earth processes
Benchmark: Knows how features on Earth's surface are constantly changed by a combination of slow and rapid processes

Wind Erosion

During the Dust Bowl of the 1930s, millions of acres of farmland became useless as a result of the drought. When the winds came, they blew away acres and acres of topsoil. Farms, homes, tractors, and even animals and people were covered with sand dunes. This effect is called wind erosion. Working in small groups, complete the following experiment on erosion.

Materials

- sand
- large tray
- cardboard box
- wooden block
- sticks, blocks, rocks, fabric, or other materials

Directions

1. Place a large tray inside a cardboard box. Cover the bottom of the tray with dry, fine sand. This is to represent the dust during the Dust Bowl. What will happen if a strong wind blows across this sand?

2. Have each person in your group take turns blowing from the same direction across the sand for a total of about 50 blows.

3. Your blows are like the wind. As it blows across the sand, it takes the sand with it. What do you think are the effects of this wind erosion?

4. Spread the sand back out again and place the wooden block in the sand. This block represents a house. Again blow the sand toward the block for at least 40 to 50 blows. What is happening?

5. What can you do to stop the sand from covering the block? Use materials such as sticks, rocks, or fabric to make a windbreak.

6. Again, blow the sand toward the block. Did your windbreak work? Compare your windbreak with those made by other groups. Did any design work? What makes a windbreak successful?

Standard: Understands basic Earth processes
Benchmark: Knows that fossils provide evidence about the plants and animals that lived long ago and about the nature of the environment at that time

How Did It Happen?

It takes many thousands of years for a rock to be formed. During this time, plants and animals die and decay, leaving behind fossil prints in the rock. Fossils are usually found in limestone.

Follow the directions below to make your own fossils. Pretend that you are an archeologist who discovered the fossils. Write a journal account describing where you uncovered the fossils and how you think the fossils may have gotten there.

Materials

- 1½-pint (.7 mL) milk carton, cleaned and dried (remove top section)

- 1 bar modeling clay

- plaster of Paris (prepared according to package directions)

- a choice of "fossil" items (shells, leaves, bones, etc.)

Directions

1. Press the modeling clay into the bottom of the carton and smooth out the top of the clay.

2. Press the chosen "fossil item" firmly into the clay and carefully remove it. This will create an impression from which to make the fossil imprint.

3. Pour a layer of the prepared plaster of Paris over the impression until it is completely covered. Set it aside to dry.

4. Tear the milk carton away from the clay and plaster. Separate the plaster from the clay.

5. You now have a fossil!

(**Note:** This type of fossil is called a "positive fossil." To create a "negative fossil" grease the top of the positive fossil with petroleum jelly and place it in a second prepared milk carton. Pour a second layer of the plaster of Paris mixture over the positive fossil until it is completely covered. Set it aside to dry. Remove the carton and separate the fossil. Now you have two different kinds of fossils!)

Standard: Knows about the diversity and unity that characterizes life
Benchmark: Knows the different ways in which living things can be grouped and the purposes of different groupings

Vertebrate and Invertebrate Animals

All animals are classified into two major groups: vertebrate and invertebrate. Vertebrate animals include all animals that have a backbone or spine. Invertebrate animals include all animals without a backbone or spine. Classify the animals below into vertebrate/invertebrate groups, and then into a subgroup; then classify them by the name of the animal, and finally by the picture of the animal. (Cut out each picture and glue it to the chart on page 61 accordingly.) Use the information in the word box to help identify the animals.

Word Box

Animal Subgroups		Animal Names	
• mammal	• insect	• dragonfly	• conch
• bird	• snail	• earthworm	• snake
• reptile	• spider	• centipede	• raccoon
• dinosaur	• crustacean	• brown spider	• catfish
• fish	• worm	• protoceratops	• lobster
• amphibian	• centipede/millipede	• duck	• frog

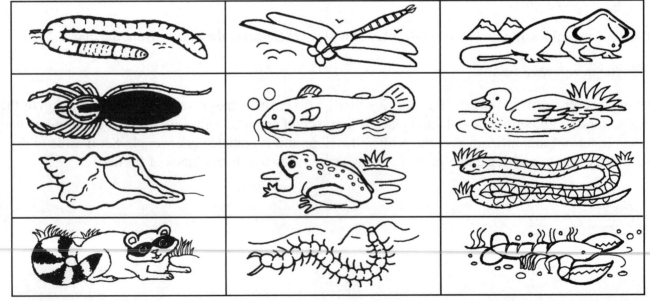

Vertebrate and Invertebrate Animals Chart

Major Group	Subgroup	Name	Picture

Standard: Understands the cycling of matter and flow of energy through the living environment
Benchmark: Knows the organization of simple food chains and food webs

Food Chain

There is a normal cycle of life for every creature on the planet. Some lives are usually very short while others are often very long. There are many factors that go into the relative lengths of lives, but one important factor is where each creature's place is on the planetary food chain.

Share with the children that the life cycles of some animals come to an end because the animal gets old. On other occasions, animals die because they are the prey (food) of other animal predators (hunters). Even though this may seem sad to the children, it is good for them to know that the cycle of predator/prey in the world is an important way for nature to keep the planet healthy and in balance. If there were too many of one kind of animal on the earth, they would take up space and resources needed by other kinds. Of course, too many animals altogether would take up the space needed by humans. Also, people are grateful that some creatures (such as insect pests) are the prey of others because these pests can destroy plants that are important food sources for people.

Let the children know that many of the animals that become prey are the weak, sick, or old. They are also usually smaller animals than the predators. The pattern of larger animal predators eating smaller animal prey is called the "food chain." The food chain tells an eating "story." For example, when asked, "What eats aphids?" the children will answer, "Ladybugs eat aphids." They know that ladybugs are bigger than aphids. When asked, "What eats ladybugs?" the children will know it is something larger than ladybugs, such as a robin or other small bird. In turn, the robin is eaten by several different four-legged animals, such as a fox, which is bigger than a robin.

To illustrate the food chain, let children complete the activity on the next page. When finished, discuss how the body of the fox, when dead, will decay and become a part of the earth. In the earth, it will nourish plants. The plants will nourish the aphids, the aphids will nourish the ladybugs, and so on. It is the "circle of life."

Materials

- a copy of page 63 for each student
- scissors
- tape

Directions

1. Color the animal strips.

2. Cut them out.

3. Glue or tape the aphids strip to make the first chain link.

4. Loop the ladybug strip through the aphids strip, showing that the ladybugs "eat" the aphids. Tape or glue the ladybugs strip, making the second link.

5. Next, add the robin strip, and finally, the fox. This shows that the robin eats the ladybugs and the fox eats the robin.

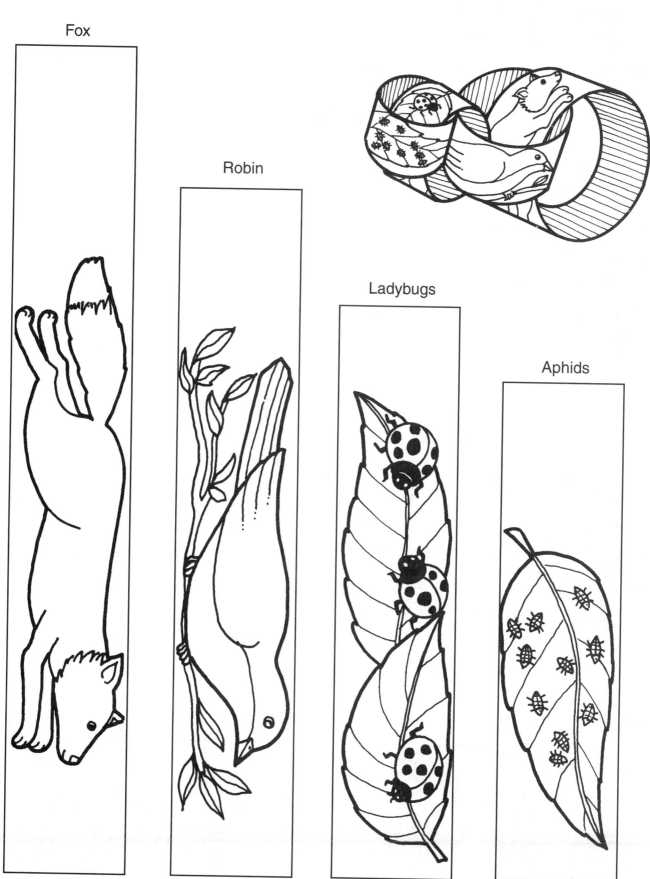

Food Chain *(cont.)*

Fox

Robin

Ladybugs

Aphids

Standard: Understands how species depend on one another and on the environment for survival

Benchmark: Knows that an organism's patterns of behavior are related to the nature of that organism's environment

Hunter and Hunted

Question

What happens to a population when there is no longer a predator?

Setting the Stage

Have students make a list of food chains that have a producer, primary consumer, secondary consumer, and top consumer. Pick one of those food chains to have the class analyze. What might happen to the population of secondary consumers if there were not top consumers? How would this impact the rest of the food chain in the short term? the long term?

Materials

- graph paper
- population statistics (page 65)
- data-capture sheet (page 66)

Directions

1. Give each student a piece of graph paper and a population statistics sheet.

2. Have students graph the two populations and then answer the questions about the graphs.

3. Discuss the relationship of the two populations with the class. Do they have any effect on each other? Why?

Extensions

- Take your class to visit a park that has a large population of deer and discuss with the park naturalist the issues faced in monitoring and controlling the deer populations.

- Have students research the life cycle of deer.

Closure

In a journal, have students describe the predator/prey relationship.

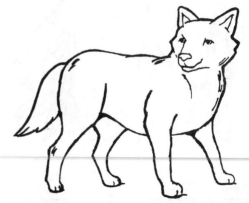

Hunter and Hunted *(cont.)*

Year	Deer Population (estimated)
1940	150
1945	180
1950	170
1955	150
1960	180
1965	200
1970	220
1975	220
1980	290
1985	320
1990	360
1995	420

Year	Wolf Population (estimated)
1940	25
1945	40
1950	40
1955	30
1960	30
1965	25
1970	25
1975	10
1980	8
1985	8
1990	3
1995	0

Hunter and Hunted *(cont.)*

1. What happened to the deer population when the wolf population increased between 1940 and 1945? Why do you think this happened?

   _____

   _____

2. Between 1960 and 1965, what happened to the deer population? What happened to the wolf population during that same time?

   _____

   _____

3. From 1975 to 1995, the deer population increased by how much?

   _____

4. From 1975 to 1995, the wolf population decreased by how much?

   _____

5. What would you have expected to happen to the wolf population from 1975–1995 as the deer population was growing?

   _____

   _____

6. What might be some causes for the deer population to increase so rapidly?

   _____

   _____

7. What might be some causes for the wolf population to decrease so rapidly?

   _____

   _____

8. What might happen if the deer population continues to grow so fast? Is there a limit to the deer population that can live on a certain area of land?

   _____

   _____

66

Standard: Knows the kinds of forces that exist between objects and within atoms

Benchmark: Knows that magnets attract and repel each other and attract certain kinds of other materials

Magnets: An Investigation

This activity can be done with the whole class, in small groups, or set up as a research center through which students are rotated.

Materials

- response sheet (page 68)

- bar and horseshoe magnets of varying strengths

- various objects, such as the following:

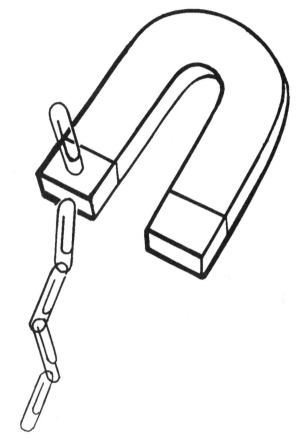

—paper clips	—plastic items
—brass fasteners	—"tin" can
—pins	—aluminum can
—ruler	—glass jar
—nails	—block of wood
—eraser	—iron filings
—bottle caps	—water
—tacks	—lightweight paper
—scissors	—piece of cloth

Directions

Have students work with the materials available to determine what a magnet will attract and what it will repel. As they collect the data, students should record it on the response sheet (page 68).

Magnets: An Investigation *(cont.)*

Response Sheet

Name _____ Date _____

Use the objects listed on page 67 to help you decide what a magnet will attract and what it will repel. Draw and label each thing you use. Talk it over with your group.

Things Magnets ATTRACT	Things Magnets REPEL

Standard: Demonstrates competence in writing scripts
Benchmark: Improvises dialogue to tell stories

Improvisation as Drama

Complete this activity after reading *Mr. Popper's Penguins* by Richard and Florence Atwater (Little Brown, 1988), or create your own scenes to assign to students based on a book you are currently reading.

Improvisational skits in the classroom allow students to relieve stress and excess energy. They can also add a bit of humor to brighten a stressful or rainy day.

The only preparation needed for this activity is a discussion of emotions and related body language. With your class, list different emotions on the board. Once this is done, ask for volunteers to demonstrate how each emotion "looks."

The next step is to explain improvisation as an acting technique. Then divide the class into small groups. Each group will go to the "stage." Give each group a situation from chapter sections 1 or 2 to act out. Their only directions will be to perform the skit, showing the different emotions. You may want to allow a short period of time to let the students assign parts and gather props.

This activity is particularly good because it will assess students' overall comprehension. Remember, it is improvisation! There is not a great deal of preparation that goes into an improvisational performance.

Here are some suggested scenes to perform from chapter sections 1 and 2:

- Mr. Popper and Captain Cook meet a neighbor on their walk.
- Captain Cook is in the barber shop.
- The service man comes to the house.
- Janie and Bill meet Captain Cook for the first time.
- The policeman talks to Mr. Popper.

After each scene is performed, ask students in the audience to identify which emotions were portrayed and how. For a little fun, the teacher may consider handing out a "Quick Thinking" award to all who participated.

Standard: Uses acting skills
Benchmark: Assumes roles that exhibit concentration and contribute to the action of dramatizations based on history

Portray a Famous Virginian

Complete this activity after reading *Misty of Chincoteague* by Marguerite Henry (Aladdin, 1999) or choose historical characters based on another book you are currently reading.

The Chincoteague ponies live in the state of Virginia. This state is famous not only for these ponies, but also for the many well-known people who are from Virginia. Some of these people lived many years ago when the Chincoteague ponies were quite new to the United States.

Option 1

Read about one of the following famous Virginians below. Dress up like that person and give a speech all about yourself as if you were that person. Include such information as the place where the person was born, what life was like in Virginia, and what contribution the person made.

- George Washington (*first president*)
- Richard Byrd (*explorer*)
- William Clark (*explorer/frontiersman*)
- William Henry Harrison (*ninth president*)
- "Stonewall" Jackson (*confederate general*)
- Thomas Jefferson (*third president*)
- John Paul Jones (*naval office*)
- Robert E. Lee (*Civil War general*)
- Cyrus Hall McCormick (*inventor*)
- Edgar Allan Poe (*poet and writer of short fiction*)
- Walter Reed (*surgeon, medical officer*)
- Zachary Taylor (*twelfth president*)
- Edward Valentine (*sculptor*)
- Booker T. Washington (*educator, author*)

Zachary Taylor

George Washington

Thomas Jefferson

Option 2

Work with a partner to develop 10 interview questions. When you have created your questions, dress up as one of the above Virginians and have your partner interview you. After you finish, you can switch places and interview him/her. Here are some sample questions:

- Where were you born?
- What was life like growing up in Virginia?
- What do you like to do in your free time?

Standard: Understands dance in various cultures and historical periods
Benchmark: Knows the cultural and/or historical context of various dances
Standard: Understands the relationship between music, history, and culture
Benchmark: Identifies music from various historical periods and cultures

Dance, Music, and Songs

During the Roaring Twenties, a dance called the jitterbug became popular in black nightclubs. It was not until the 1940s, though, that it became the rage as it caught on with the white teenage culture. An athletic dance, it featured fancy footwork and even airborne steps in which the male would swing his female partner over his head and between his legs. Although many adults disapproved of the dance—they felt it was too physical and uninhibited—there was no stopping it. In fact, the jitterbug grew into an international craze when U.S. servicemen introduced the dance to England and the rest of Europe.

The typical female jitterbuggers of World War II wore white socks that covered the ankles, saddle shoes, and heavy makeup to look older. Nicknamed "bobbysoxers," they danced in the canteens where soldiers who were on leave went for entertainment. Jitterbuggers danced to any number of popular hits, including Glenn Miller's "Chattanooga Choo Choo" and "In the Mood" and the Andrew Sisters' "Boogie Woogie Bugle Boy."

Most big bands had one or more vocalists, and their vocals were also a hit. One singer, Frances Albert Sinatra, became the idol of the bobbysoxers. More commonly known as Frank Sinatra, he started his singing career as a vocalist with the big band of Harry James in 1939. Girls attending his performances screamed and swooned as he sang his ballads. Bing Crosby was another favorite crooner and actor of the era. In the 1942 movie *Holiday Inn*, he sang "White Christmas," which became one of the most popular songs ever.

Suggested Activities

Dance: Watch a dance sequence from a 1940s movie to see how the jitterbug was done, or invite a dance instructor to set up a classroom demonstration.

Sinatra: Frank Sinatra went on to become a movie star, too. Make a list of some movies in which he appeared. Write a list of the '40s tunes he made popular. Listen to some of his early music. An excellent resource is *Frank Sinatra: The Best of the Columbia Years.* This four-CD set from Columbia/Legacy covers his singing career from 1943–1952.

Big Band: Listen to some Big Band music. Check your local music store or library for tapes, records, or CDs. One title to look for is *Big Band Renaissance: The Evolution of Jazz Orchestra—the 1940s and Beyond.* This set is from Smithsonian and includes 5 CDs (also available in cassette form).

Frank Sinatra

WWII Songs: Make a list of some popular World War II songs. Listen to some typical '40s music. *Command Performance Radio Show Collection* and *We'll Meet Again: The Smithsonian Collection of World War II Love Songs* from the Wireless catalogue (800-669-9999) feature original recordings of the era.

Standard: Knows and applies appropriate criteria to music and music performances

Benchmark: Identifies the sounds of a variety of instruments

Sergei Prokofiev

Born in the Ukraine on April 23, 1891, Sergei Prokofiev (Pruh-KAWF-yev) demonstrated his musical ability from an early age. When he was four, he began studying piano with his mother. He composed his first piano work at five. He wrote an opera by age nine, a symphony by age twelve, and won composition prizes as a teenager. During his teen years, he enrolled at the St. Petersburg conservatory. He wrote many compositions while there, including his first two piano concertos. By the time Prokofiev graduated in 1914, he was a "controversial" figure because his compositions were so dissonant (or harsh to the ear).

Because of the revolutionary times in Russia, Prokofiev left for the United States in 1918. He premiered some of his greatest works while there—his *Third Piano Concerto* and the opera, *Love for Three Oranges*—and he was appreciated and well-respected. In the 1920s, he moved to Paris and continued to compose.

Prokofiev stayed in Paris until 1936, the same year in which he composed *Peter and the Wolf,* a story for a narrator and orchestra. He returned to what was then the Soviet Union and settled in Moscow, Russia. Because he was now supported by the government, he realized he needed to compose for a wide audience. He created such memorable works as *Romeo and Juliet* and *Cinderella* for ballet; the *Fifth Symphony*; film scores, such as *Ivan the Terrible*; and operas, including the dramatic *War and Peace*.

Quite often, the compositions Prokofiev wrote throughout his career were filled with humor, charm, beautiful melodies, rhythmic vitality, percussive instrumentation, imagination, and purpose. He attracted a wide, appreciative audience. He also was a talented pianist and frequently performed his own concertos and piano solos.

In 1948, Soviet officials thought Prokofiev's music was too dissonant, too unharmonious. They accused him of composing without the ideals of the Communist Party in mind. These later years were filled with illness and frustration. He died of a stroke on March 5, 1953. He had been the leading Russian composer of his time.

Sergei Prokofiev *(cont.)*

Peter, the Wolf, and Others!

Do you ever think that instruments you hear sound like characters in a story? What characters might sound like flutes or violins? Which ones might sound like trombones, tubas, or bassoons? What would a dragon, a prince, or a fairy sound like?

Sergei Prokofiev enjoyed matching instruments with characters in a musical story called *Peter and the Wolf.* Listen to the story told by a narrator and the orchestra. As each character is introduced with an instrument, try to recognize its sound and melody.

Activity

After listening to the music, match each of the instruments below to the character it represents. Use the names in the Character Box to help you.

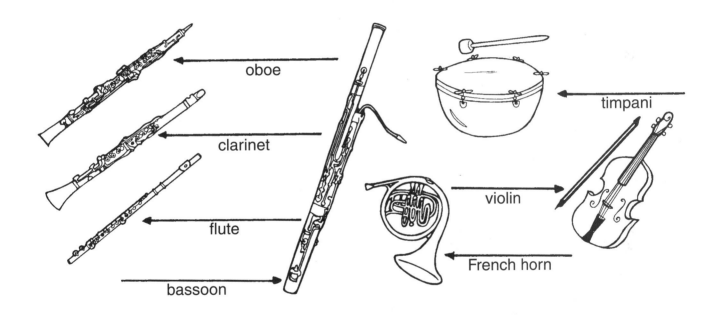

Character Box

Peter	Grandfather	hunters	wolf
cat	bird	duck	

After listening to *Peter and the Wolf,* do each of the following activities.

1. Make a short summary of the story in words and/or pictures.

2. List 10 different animals and the instruments you think would best represent them.

3. Think of a familiar story. List the characters in the story and the instruments that could be used to represent them.

Standard: Sings, alone and with others, a varied repertoire of music
Benchmark: Knows songs representing genres and styles from diverse cultures

Yippi Ti Yi Yea!

Complete this activity after reading *Little House on the Prairie* by Laura Ingalls Wilder (Harper & Row 1971).

Singing and music are mentioned throughout the book *Little House on the Prairie.* Pa's fiddle playing is both a comfort and entertainment for Laura. It is a way for Pa and Mr. Edwards to relax after a hard day's labor. Even the cowboys and the Indians have their own songs. Here is your chance to learn one of those songs and teach it to your classmates! Then you can do what the Ingalls family and other people of their time did for fun long before TV, movies, and video games existed—get together and sing!

Work in groups of four or five for this project!

1. Find the lyrics and music for an old pioneer, cowboy, or translated Indian song that the group likes. This can be one of the songs mentioned in the novel or an old folk song like "Oh, Susanna" or "My Darling Clementine" or "Bury Me Not on the Lone Prairie," etc. As soon as you have made your choice, let your teacher know what song you want to do. No two groups should do the same song.

2. Become familiar enough with the lyrics that you can teach them to your classmates. Find a place (hallway, cafeteria, etc.) where you can practice singing the song together.

3. Decide how you will accompany your song. Does one of your group play the piano, a guitar, or some other instrument? Can he/she play the melody? Can some (or all) of the members of your group tap or clap out the rhythm of the song while you sing? Can you locate a recording of the song that you could play for the class before you ask them to sing it? Practice again, using some kind of accompaniment.

4. Decide who will be your song leader. One person might lead the whole song while the others in the group sing behind him/her. Or, you might take turns, each member or a pair of members leading a different stanza of the song. Practice!

5. Have the teacher make enough copies of your song that you can give them to your classmates.

It's Sing Along Time! (Put the titles of all the songs in a box.)

6. If you have the space (outside in nice weather, in the gym, etc.), sit in a big circle, campfire style.

7. The teacher will draw one title at a time from the box. As your title is called, your group will pass out copies of your song, go to the "front" of the campfire, demonstrate your song, then lead the class in singing it once or twice. (If you know anything special about your song, share it with the group before you sing.)

Standard: Improvises melodies, variations, and accompaniments
Benchmark: Improvises short songs and instrumental pieces using a variety of sound sources

It's Instrumental

A successful inventor looks at an object and sees that it can have more than one function. Several glasses filled with different levels of water can serve as a musical scale for playing a favorite song.

Create a new instrument, using materials commonly found around the home or at school. Decide how you will assemble them to make an instrument that will produce sound. Draw your design in the box below. Label the parts of the instrument. At the bottom of the page, write a brief explanation of how to play your instrument.

Share your instrument invention with the class. Or, combine several instrument inventions to form your own band!

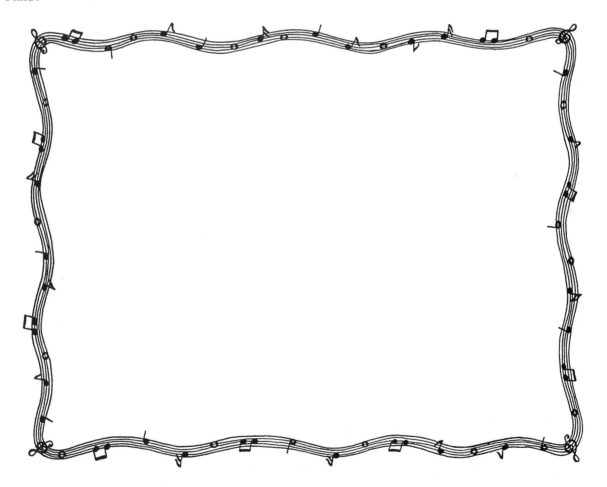

Standard: Improvises melodies, variations, and accompaniments
Benchmark: Improvises short songs and instrumental pieces using a variety of sound sources

Having Fun with the Scales

It is likely that Do, Re, Mi, Fa, So, La, Ti, and Do are familiar to you. The notes they represent are called the notes of the musical scale, and its notes are the basic components of all musical arrangements.

For the movie *The Sound of Music*, Rodgers and Hammerstein wrote a song that rearranges those notes. At one point the characters sing, for example, "Do, Mi, Mi / Mi, So, So / Re, Fa, Fa / La, Ti, Ti." This was the way the lead character had of teaching the other characters how to sing. She sang, "When you know the notes to sing / You can sing most anything." She's right.

Learn and study the notes of the musical scale. Become familiar with each. Now, have some fun with them! Cut out all the notes at the bottom of the page. (The second "Do" represents the highest note; there is an asterisk marked next to it.) Rearrange them in any order you like, gluing them down. Remember, you have the freedom to choose, so do anything you want! Now practice singing your new arrangement. Can you do it? Can someone else sing it with you and carry the same tune? Now try singing someone else's tune. Do your new songs sound "right," or do they sound strange? Can you rearrange them differently to make them sound better? Would you like to add or delete any notes? Give it a try.

Do	Do	Do	Do	Do	Do	Do
Re	Re	Re	Re	Re	Re	Re
Mi	Mi	Mi	Mi	Mi	Mi	Mi
Fa	Fa	Fa	Fa	Fa	Fa	Fa
So	So	So	So	So	So	So
La	La	La	La	La	La	La
Ti	Ti	Ti	Ti	Ti	Ti	Ti
Do*	Do*	Do*	Do*	Do*	Do*	Do*

Standard: Knows and applies appropriate criteria to music and music performances

Benchmark: Knows appropriate terminology used to explain music, music notation, music instruments and voices, and music performances

Franz Joseph Haydn

The composer known as the "Father of the Symphony" was born in a small Austrian village called Rohrau on March 31, 1732. Early on, the Haydns realized that their young son had musical talent, so when a cousin offered to train him in a nearby city, the parents agreed. At six years old, young Joseph Haydn (HIGH-den) moved away from home.

When he was eight, Haydn's excellent voice brought him to the attention of a court composer. In 1740, he was admitted to a boarding school where singers were trained for the emperor's court in Vienna. While he was there, Joseph Haydn received an academic education. The boy continued his studies of the violin and harpsicord and began to compose music. But when he was 17, his voice changed and he was dismissed from the school.

Times were not easy for Haydn. When he left the school, he had no money. While styling wigs as a barber's helper, he earned enough money to rent a place of his own. He became a music teacher and wrote his first Mass. Haydn later worked for several years as a composer and music director for a count. In 1761, Haydn began work for Prince Esterhazy in Austria, and soon, he was put in charge of all court music. There he remained, composing for almost 30 years.

Haydn met Wolfgang Amadeus Mozart in 1781, and the two became close friends, learning from and encouraging each other until Mozart's death in 1791.

From 1791 to 1794, Haydn wrote his last 12 symphonies, called the *London Symphonies*, while in England. One of the most famous of these is the *Surprise Symphony*. In it, he gave the audience a big surprise during the slow movement—the bangs of loud kettle drums to awaken anyone who was sleeping!

Franz Joseph Haydn composed more than 100 symphonies. He is probably most renowned for his transformation of the symphony from a short and simple form into a long form requiring a large orchestra. Haydn's combination of instruments in his orchestra formed the basis for modern symphonic orchestras.

His composition was not limited to symphonies. He wrote over 80 string quartets; and, in many of these quartets, the two violins, a viola, and a cello seem to talk to each other. Some of the most famous string quartets are "The Bird," "Sunrise," and "Emperor." Haydn also wrote two of his greatest works, *The Creation* and *The Seasons* for solo vocalists, a large chorus, and orchestra. This talented musician also found time to keep on teaching. One of his promising students was Ludwig van Beethoven!

Haydn, along with composers such as Mozart, Beethoven, and Tchaikovsky, earned his place in history as a master of the symphonic form.

Franz Joseph Haydn *(cont.)*

What Is an Orchestra?

Haydn needed a talented orchestra to perform his symphonic works of art. An orchestra is a large group of musicians playing different musical instruments under the direction of a conductor. An orchestra may be large or small, depending on the needs of the composer who has written the piece to be performed.

The four main families of instruments that make up an orchestra are strings, woodwinds, brass, and percussion. If possible, listen to examples of each of the instruments. Many fine recordings are available.

For a live performance, each of the instruments is placed in a specific location, according to a generally accepted format. This format has been accepted to help balance and blend the sounds of the instruments so that the audience will get the full effect of the composer's intent. For example, the stringed instruments are seated in front of the percussion and brass sections, because they are softer sounding and could be overpowered by the beating of drums, the clashing of cymbals, and the blaring of trumpets. The woodwinds are grouped together so that their sound will blend as one.

Activity: Locate information and illustrations showing the arrangement of musicians in an orchestra. Use the materials you obtained and the diagram below to indicate the placement of the four main families of instruments in an orchestra. (You may draw a picture of the instrument or write its name in the appropriate section.) Compare your completed diagram with other students' arrangements. Are they exactly alike? If they are different, in what sections were changes made?

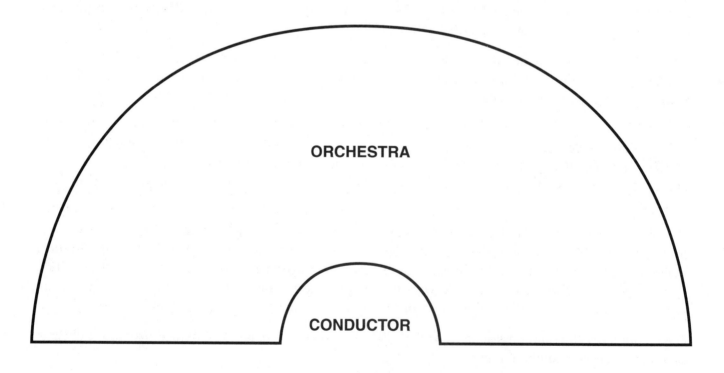

Standard: Understands the relationship between music and history and culture

Benchmark: Understands the roles of musicians in various music settings and cultures

Peter Ilich Tchaikovsky

Acknowledged as the greatest composer in Russia and one of the great composers in the world, Peter Ilich Tchaikovsky (chi-KAWF-skee) was truly a composer for the people. Great masses of people throughout the world, not just the rich and privileged, listened to his music. His music reflected not only his own powerful emotions and his Russian patriotism, but also feelings that were (and are) common to all of humanity.

On May 7, 1840, Peter Ilich Tchaikovsky was born in a Ural Mountains settlement in Russia, where his father was a mining inspector. His mother sang many types of songs to him, from folk songs to operatic arias. He began playing piano at age five; he loved to play. When Peter was eight, his family moved to St. Petersburg, a place where Peter could be exposed to a rich cultural and educational background. He spent much of his time composing songs on his piano. His parents didn't think he could earn a living in music, so they sent him to a school to prepare him for a service in the government.

As his parents wished, Peter grew up to become a law clerk for the government. He relegated music to a hobby. Eventually, Tchaikovsky left his job and began to study music in St. Petersburg full time when he was 23. When he graduated, he began to teach music at the Moscow conservatory. Peter continued to do so for about 12 years, until his life was changed by a wealthy woman named Nadeszhda von Meck. She loved his music and agreed to support him so he could spend all his time composing music. They were never to meet, but they wrote letters faithfully to one another for many years.

Tchaikovsky's compositions are many and varied; they included symphonies, symphonic poems, operas, concertos, ballets, songs, and other works. His work is dramatic and filled with emotion. Many of his pieces reflect the influence of Russian folk music. He also developed quite a reputation as a traveler, conducting orchestras in many countries other than his native Russia.

Tchaikovsky loved Russia, although there were things about it that bothered him. He saw the harsh contrast between the lives of the ruling class and the rest of the people. His music served well to bring these people together, instead of pointing out their differences. He loved humanity, consistently showing a concern for others, regardless of their position in life. The composer also loved children. Many youngsters, both of his own family and not, called him Uncle Peter.

Shortly after conducting the premiere of his *Sixth Symphony*, he died in St. Petersburg on November 6, 1893. Many if his creations, especially his *1812 Overture*, remain among the most recognizable pieces of music in the world today.

Peter Ilich Tchaikovsky *(cont.)*

All Together, Now!

Whenever a musician plays with one or more musicians at a time, he or she needs to know a few things. "When do I start, or how do I attack the music?" "At what volume, or dynamic level, should I play?" and "How fast, or at what tempo, should I play?"

In some types of music, the players can follow the beat of a drummer, but not all music works that way.

A conductor is often needed to make sure all musicians know when, what, and how to play. Although every conductor has his or her own personal style of conducting, there is a basic pattern that most follow.

Activity: Learn some of the basics of conducting with the following activity. Use your right hand, a conductor's baton, or a pencil to reproduce the basic conducting pattern. Make the pattern bigger when you want the sound to be louder. Use your left hand to tell the musicians when to be ready to come in. Follow the pattern below as you listen to a piece of music (in 4/4 time) by Tchaikovsky. As you follow the pattern, count to yourself: 1 and 2 and 3 and 4.

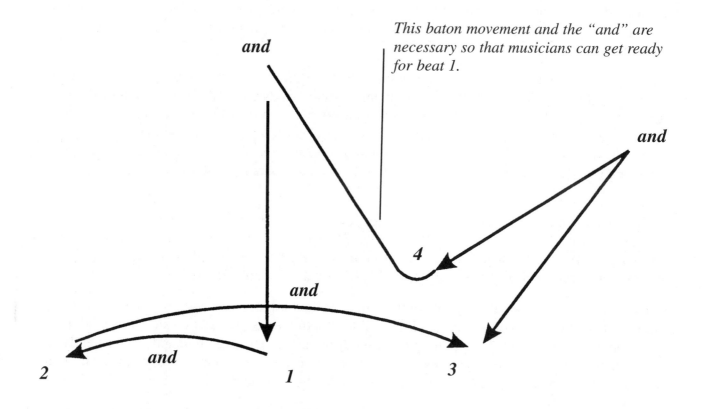

Conducting an orchestra takes a special talent. A conductor must know the music, the talents of the musicians in the orchestra, and the composer's desires. He or she must make sure the sounds are balanced and blended and that the music is played the way the composer intended for it to be played. Tchaikovsky conducted throughout the world, traveling by boat to places as far away as the United States. As both a conductor and a composer, he was in great demand.

Standard: Knows a range of subject matter, symbols, and potential ideas in the visual arts
Benchmark: Selects prospective ideas for works of art

Modern Art

The primary purpose of art is to express yourself, not to please others, so choose mediums (e.g., painting, poetry, music, sculpture, etc.) that appeal to you. You are going to create your own artwork.

Now that you have chosen a medium, you will need a subject. (Perhaps you will wish to choose your subject first and then your medium. That is all right, too.) To decide upon a subject, a good way to begin is to get in touch with your feelings right now. Art and feelings are both creative, and therefore work hand in hand. Read over the list of feelings below, and circle any that appeal to you now.

afraid	embarrassed	overwhelmed
angry	enraged	peaceful
anxious	exhausted	playful
apprehensive	frightened	puzzled
ashamed	frustrated	sad
bewildered	guilty	serene
bored	happy	shocked
calm	hopeful	shy
cautious	hysterical	silly
clumsy	jealous	smug
confident	joyful	surprised
confused	lonely	suspicious
depressed	lovesick	terrified
disgusted	lovestruck	tired
ecstatic	quarrelsome	uptight
edgy	mischievous	worried

Let your art be an extension of the feelings you selected. On the back of this page, brainstorm subjects that fit your "feeling" description. The subjects must come entirely from you. Although a subject calls forth a certain feeling for you, it may call forth a different response from someone else.

Finally, create your work of art using the medium(s), feeling(s), and subject(s) you've chosen. Remember, art is for your own expression! You don't have to please anyone else.

Standard: Knows how to use structures and functions of art
Benchmark: Knows some of the various visual structures and functions of art

Carousel Horses

Masterpiece: "Circus" by Georges Seurat

Concept: Animals

Objectives

A. The students will expand their drawing skills.

B. The students will create a decorative horse using line, color, shape, and patterns.

Vocabulary

- carousel
- color
- line
- shape
- pattern

Materials

- 18" x 24" (46 cm x 61 cm) tagboard
- pencils
- brushes
- tempera paint
- thick black markers (or black tempera)
- picture of a carousel horse (See page 83.)

Process

1. Give each student an example of a carousel horse. This will be used as a source picture for their drawings. Encourage them to change, add, or combine parts to create their own style of horse.

2. Draw the basic horse shape on the 18" x 24" (46 cm x 61 cm) tagboard.

3. Add details to this horse: saddle, reins, fringe, straps, etc.

4. Paint areas with tempera paint. You may leave your horse the white color of the paper.

5. Let paint dry.

6. Outline objects with a black marker or a thin brush and black tempera.

7. Cut out horses. You may add a striped pole to your horse.

Evaluation

A. Did the student understand the concept introduced?

B. Did the student handle the media correctly?

C. Did the student use his/her creativity to complete a decorative horse?

Carousel Horses *(cont.)*

Familiar Teaching Methods and Standards

Meeting standards does not mean that we have to throw out good teaching strategies we already use. Below are some familiar teaching methods. Take a look at how standards can be met using learning centers, technology, and multiple intelligences.

Learning Centers

A learning center is an area in the classroom where one or more children can participate in activities designed for enrichment and reinforcement of the skills being taught. A learning center coordinated with the curriculum enhances those skills and learning. Rather than serve as primary instruction, a learning center supports what is taught in the classroom. A center provides an alternative to the traditional concept of seat work. It allows the student an opportunity to independently practice skills and assume responsibility for learning, while freeing the teacher to work with small groups or individual students. An example of how learning centers can meet standards is provided on pages 85–91. Set up around the theme of measurement, these four activity stations cover topics such as area, perimeters, and working with rulers.

Technology

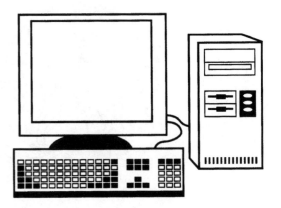

Computers are so much a part of people's lives that it is almost impossible to consider life without them. They have even become an essential part of the school day. Teachers and administrators have set the goal of preparing students to be technologically literate. But research and experience have shown that hands-on use of technology will likely have little long-term impact on student learning and skills development unless it is accompanied by materials and activities that provide a broader context, perspective, and application for the use of technology skills. This is an excellent reason to use technology as a tool to help children meet standards. By coupling these fields together, students can learn essential technology skills, as well as become competent in curriculum standards. An example of how technology and standards can work together is provided on pages 92–93. In this activity, students are able to use a computer and the Internet to learn more about the water cycle.

Multiple Intelligences

There are many reasons for addressing multiple intelligences in your classroom. Once you have determined the intelligences of the students in your class, you can enrich and cultivate each individual's dominant intelligences, strengthen the weaker ones, or just allow everyone to experience all of them. Examples are provided on pages 94–104 which demonstrate how standards and the intelligences can both be addressed in the same activity.

Standard: Understands and applies basic and advanced properties of the concepts of measurement
Benchmarks: Understands the basic measures—perimeter, area, volume, capacity, mass, angle, and circumference; understands relationships between measures

Working with Rulers

During the following activities, students will be working with measurement, perimeter, and area. They will be creating their own metric rulers and measuring items commonly found in the classroom.

Materials

- computer
- rulers
- Measuring My Stuff sheet (page 87)
- Finding the Perimeter sheet (page 89)
- Finding the Area sheet (page 91)

Software

- Claris Works, MS Works, or other drawing program

Internet Link

- http://www.svusd.k12.ca.us/curriculum//Eighth/Tech8/math.html

Activity #1

Before the Computer:

- If students have a printer and a drawing program, they can create their own metric ruler for use in the following activities. If not, they can still do the activities using a metric ruler.
- Students should have an understanding of the difference between metric units of measurement and standard measurement, which is still used in the United States. Stress that the United States is one of only a few countries still relying on this older way of measuring and that the metric system is much easier to work with.
- Since the very first activity is to create a metric ruler, it would be a good idea to have a printer connected to your computer that will print exactly what is seen on the computer screen. Generally, any ink jet or laser printer is capable of printing screen captures; some older printers are not.

On the Computer:

- Students should start the drawing application and turn on the ruler function. If they are using MS Works, they can find the ruler function in the pulldown menu under View.
- They will need to change the measurement units on the ruler. The drawing page will be in inches since this is the unit most commonly used. If they are working with ClarisWorks, they would find Rulers under the Format pulldown menu.
- Set the units to centimeters. If students get stuck at this step and do not know where to make these changes, ask one of the classroom experts for help.
- They should now see rulers in centimeters on both the top and left or right edge, depending on which program is being used.
- Most drawing programs have a View button. This button, which can be found in a menu, will allow students to shrink or enlarge the screen. Shrink (or scale) the picture to 50%. This will allow them to see the entire page, and that will make drawing the ruler much easier.
- They are going to be drawing a ruler that is 4 cm wide and 20 cm long. (See page 86.)

Working with Rulers *(cont.)*

On the Computer: *(cont.)*

- This screen shot shows the three steps needed in order to make a metric ruler. First, students should draw a rectangle that is 4 cm wide and 20 cm long.

- Next, add divisions that are 2 cm apart. If the program they are using has an autogrid function, use it to draw the lines.

- Finally, draw lines at 1-cm intervals. They will notice that on the left-hand ruler, the first number found is 4. They will also see that on the ruler they are creating, there are 4 cm when they reach this point.

- After they have completed marking off all the 1-cm intervals on the ruler, they can label it. This can be done either before printing or after printing.

- Student rulers should measure exactly 20 cm. They may want to check it against another metric ruler in the classroom.

Activity #2

Finding the Measurement:

- Students are now ready to measure a variety of items in the classroom. The following is a list of items that they will be measuring. Before starting, make some predictions about how many centimeters these items are. Use page 87 for the predictions. Students may want to devise a plan that they can use to measure items that are more than 20 cm long.

a. their math books	f. their shoes
b. their pencils	g. any ball
c. the tops of their desks	h. a crayon
d. their little fingers	i. a piece of binder paper
e. the chalkboard	

Measuring My Stuff

```
|1   2   3   4   5   6   7   8   9   10  11  12  13  14  15|
```

- Using the ruler that you created in the previous activity, measure these objects. Fill in the chart below as you go along. When you are done measuring all of the objects, fill in the assessment questions.

   a. your math book
   b. your pencil
   c. the top of your desk

   d. your little finger
   e. the chalkboard
   f. your shoe

   g. any ball
   h. a crayon
   i. a piece of binder paper

Item	Predicted Size	Actual Size
a. your math book ⟶		
b. your pencil ⟶		
c. the top of your desk ⟶		
d. your little finger ⟶		
e. the chalkboard ⟶		
f. your shoe ⟶		
g. any ball ⟶		
h. a crayon ⟶		
i. a piece of binder paper ⟶		

Assessment:

This is a self-assessment activity. You should answer the following questions about this activity:

1. What part of the activity did you find most difficult?_____

_____

2. How many of the items were larger than 20 cm? What did you have to do in order to measure these items?

_____

_____

3. Do you think that everyone doing this activity will come up with the same kind of results that you did? Why or why not?

_____

_____

Finding the Perimeter

Activity #3

Before the Computer:

- Since this activity uses some parts of the first two activities (found on pages 85–87), it is important that students either do Activities 1 and 2 first, or understand what was done.

- In Activity 3, they will be working with the concept of perimeter. You may want to do a quick review of what the term *perimeter* means. For the purpose of this activity, students will only be working with shapes that have straight lines for sides. Shapes, like the square and rectangle, allow for shortcuts to find the perimeter because some or all of the sides are equal. Students should notice that only one measurement was needed for the square, since all sides are equal. In each sample pictured here, the sides were measured and then totaled.

- The examples show students how to calculate the perimeter of a number of different shapes. In the following activities, they will not only be measuring the perimeter of items, but they will also be creating shapes on the computer with a specific perimeter.

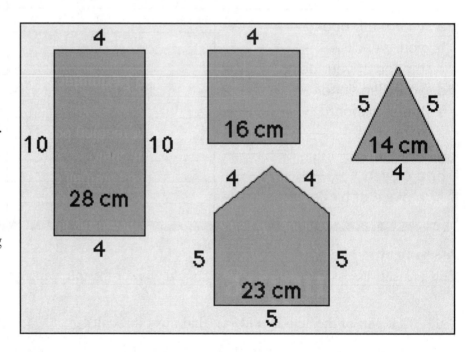

- The unit of measurement that was used here is the centimeter, the same unit that students will be using.

On the Computer:

- Since some of the objects or spaces students will be measuring will be greater than 20 cm, they are going to enlarge their rulers. If students have forgotten how to make a 20 cm ruler, they should go back to page 86.

- How many centimeters equal one meter? How many 20-cm rulers will be needed to make a ruler that is 100 cm long? Students can print five 20-cm rulers and then tape them end-to-end. They can label the intervals in any way that works for them, either before printing the 20 cm rulers or after. Teachers should point out that a one-meter ruler is just a few inches longer than a yardstick (which is three feet long).

Finding the Perimeter:

- When students have completed the steps above, they are ready to find the perimeter of some commonly found objects or places. They should fill out the form on page 89 with their predictions and actual results. If students are not clear about what they are supposed to do, have them ask one of the classroom experts for help.

Finding the Perimeter *(cont.)*

- Using the ruler that you created on the previous page, measure these objects. Fill in the chart below as you go along. When you are done measuring all of the objects, fill in the assessment questions.

a. your classroom	d. the basketball court	g. your teacher's desk
b. your desk	e. your chair	h. your foot
c. the chalkboard	f. your reading book	i. a piece of paper

Item	Predicted Perimeter	Actual Perimeter
a. your classroom ⟶		
b. your desk ⟶		
c. the chalkboard ⟶		
d. the basketball court ⟶		
e. your chair ⟶		
f. your reading book ⟶		
g. your teacher's chair ⟶		
h. your foot ⟶		
i. a piece of paper ⟶		
j. your choice ⟶		
_____		

Assessment:

This is a self assessment activity. You should answer the following questions about this activity.

1. What part of the activity did you find most difficult?_____

_____

2. How many of the items were larger than one meter? What did you have to do in order to measure these items?

_____

_____

3. Do you think that everyone doing this activity will come up with the same kind of results that you did? Why or why not?

_____

_____

Finding the Area

Activity #4

Before the Computer:

- In the previous activity, students learned that they could find the perimeter of an object by adding up the distance around that object. In this final activity, they will find the area of some of the items from the previous list. In order to do this, they will once again need the 100 cm, or 1 meter, ruler.

- With the students, go over the concept of finding the area of a space. In the examples below, some of the shapes require that the students multiply more than once and then add the results together. This is how the area of a home would be measured.

- These three examples may help students with the concept of how the area of a shape is found. The area is the space within a shape.

- In order to find the area of a square or a rectangle, students should multiply one side by the adjacent side. This will tell them how many square centimeters the shape is. They would label this answer 24 sq. centimeters.

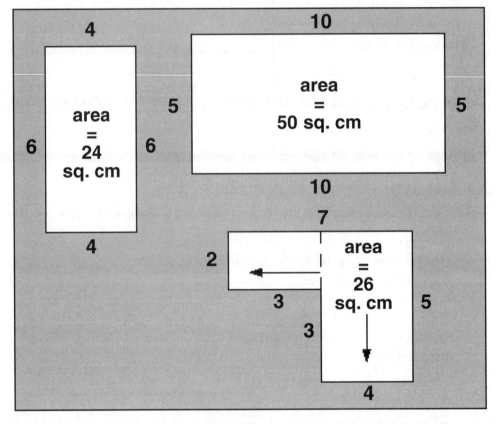

- The third shape is a little different. There are two different rectangular parts to this shape, and one way students can find its area is to find the area of each part and then add the two together. This is what was done to find the area of this shape. First, the smaller left part was found to be 3 x 2 = 6 sq. cm. Then the larger right part was found to be 5 x 4 = 20 sq. cm. When added together, 20 sq. cm and 6 sq. cm total 26 sq. cm.

- Shapes such as triangles and those with irregular sides, such as a pentagon, are more difficult to calculate the area.

Finding the Area *(cont.)*

Finding the Area:

- Find the area of some of the shapes with which you have previously worked. If you did not do the previous two activities, then you will need to take the measurements of these items first.

- Find the area of the following shapes or spaces:

  a. your desk   d. your classroom

  b. the blackboard   e. one of the books in your desk

  c. a piece of paper

ITEM	Predicted Area	Actual Area
a. your desk ⟶		
b. the blackboard ⟶		
c. a piece of paper ⟶		
d. your classroom ⟶		
e. a book ⟶		

Assessment:

This is a self-assessment activity. You should answer the following questions about this activity.

1. What part of the activity did you find most difficult?_____

   _____

   _____

2. Do you think that everyone doing this activity will come up with the same kind of results that you did? Why or why not?

   _____

   _____

   _____

Follow-up Activities:

- Is there a way that you can find the area of a triangle using measurement? Here is a hint. Study this little drawing for a minute.

- Some shapes have the exact same number for the perimeter and the area.

- An example would be a square whose sides are 4 cm. This would give it a perimeter of 16 cm and an area of 16 sq. cm. Can you think of any other examples where this is true?

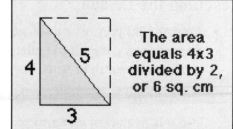

The area equals 4x3 divided by 2, or 6 sq. cm

Standard: Understands basic features of Earth
Benchmark: Knows the processes involved in the water cycle

Cycle of Water

Content Area

Earth science

Objectives

Students will . . .

- identify the parts of the water cycle.

- determine the role of transpiration in the water cycle.

- analyze the cycle and determine the amount of water on Earth now as compared with 100,000 years ago.

Materials

- computer with Internet access

- pencil or pen

- copies of page 93

Web Sites

- http://www.mobot.org/MBGnet/fresh/cycle/index.htm

- http://www.mobot.org/MBGnet/fresh/cycle/concepts.htm

- http://www.mobot.org/MBGnet/fresh/cycle.htm

Time

- approximately 25–35 minutes

Teaching the Lesson

- An essential part of any science curriculum, this concept is one of which students must take ownership if they are to understand why polluting their own sinks or storm drain affects all of the creatures on earth in some way.

- This activity is for individuals or pairs of students.

- Use this as part of an earth science, ecology, or recycling unit.

Cycle of Water *(cont.)*

Name: _____ **Date:** _____

Where does the water you use for drinking and bathing purposes come from? The water cycle, of course. Chances are the water you use was used by someone or something else at some time—but don't worry, because the water cycle cleans our water, too.

Go to ***http://www.mobot.org/MBGnet/fresh/cycle/index/htm***

Read the Web page about the water cycle. Complete the questions below.

1. How much of the earth's water is fresh water? _____

    Go to ***http://www.mobot.org/MBGnet/fresh/cycle/concepts/htm***

2. What causes *evaporation*? _____
    _____
    _____

3. Why is evaporated water especially clean? _____
    _____
    _____

4. What is another name for *precipitation*? _____
    _____
    _____

5. Where does *transpiration* happen? _____

    Go to ***http://www.mobot.org/MBGnet/fresh/cycle/cycle.htm***

6. What are the four parts of the water cycle? _____
    _____
    _____

7. How much water is there on earth today compared with 100,000 years ago?
    _____

Intelligence: Verbal/Linguistic   **Curricular Area:** Language Arts

Standard: Demonstrates competence in the general skills and strategies for reading a variety of literary texts

Benchmark: Applies reading skills and strategies to a variety of literary passages and texts

How to Read a Poem

If you want to write poems that you and others will enjoy reading, you will need to strengthen your "poetic ear." When you have a poetic ear, you can enjoy and appreciate reading and writing poetry. To strengthen your poetic ear, you need to read lots of poetry—and write it, too.

Here is a very famous poem by the American poet Robert Frost. Read this poem and other poems by following the list of directions at the bottom of the page. After you've done this with a few poems, you will start to notice that your poetic ear is getting stronger.

Stopping by the Woods on a Snowy Evening

Whose woods these are I think I know.

His house is in the village though;

He will not see me stopping here

To watch his woods fill up with snow.

My little horse must think it queer

To stop without a farmhouse near

Between the woods and frozen lake

The darkest evening of the year.

He gives his harness bells a shake

To ask if there is some mistake.

The only other sound's the sweep

Of easy wind and downy flake.

The woods are lovely, dark and deep

But I have promises to keep,

And miles to go before I sleep,

And miles to go before I sleep.

First, read the poem carefully all the way through. Next, read the poem aloud. When you read a poem, pay more attention to the punctuation than to the ends of lines. If there is no punctuation, go right to the next line as you read just as you would for a sentence in a story. Listen to it as you read.

Extension: Write this poem on a piece of art paper and illustrate it. Choose several poems you like and write them in a poetry journal where you can collect your favorites.

Intelligence: Bodily/Kinesthetic **Curricular Area:** Social Studies

Standard: Understands the history of a local community and how communities in North America varied long ago

Benchmark: Knows geographical settings, economic activities, food, clothing, homes, crafts, and rituals of Native American societies long ago

Native American Games

(**Note:** Danger Signal should be played outdoors; the others can be played indoors or outdoors.)

Tossing and Catching Games

Bowl Catch *(variations found in all areas of the Americas)*

The Native Americans played this game with a bowl and pottery disks, beaver or muskrat teeth, fruit pits, or bone depending on the area. One side of the object was plain, and the other had designs which established its value.

Materials

- shallow basket (8"–10" or 20 cm to 25 cm across)
- 6 large lima beans

Directions

With a marker draw a Native American symbol on one side of each bean. Put the beans in the bowl. Sitting cross-legged, hold the bowl in both hands. Toss the beans into the air. Catch them in the bowl. Count those that land design side up, this is your score. Depending on the age and ability of the students, the symbols can be assigned a value and it can become a math game.

Toss and Catch *(played by Plains, Woodlands, and Northwest Coast tribes)*

Materials

- sticks or reeds 3"–4" (7.5 to 10 cm) long and ⅛"–¼" (.3 to .6 cm) in diameter

Directions

Balance two craft sticks on the back of your hand at waist level. Toss the sticks straight up into the air to about the height of your head and catch them in the palm of your hand. To increase difficulty, add more sticks, turn around before catching the sticks, or catch the sticks with your palm open.

Hunting and Stalking Game

Danger Signal *(played by Plains, Woodlands, and Northwest Coast tribes)*

To develop hunting skills, young braves were taken into a fairly dense forest and told to spread out in various directions. They were told to listen for danger signals such as those given by alarmed birds or animals. At the sound of the alarm, they were to freeze or head quickly for the cover of a tree or rock. Divide the class into thirds: braves, rocks, trees. Position yourself (as chief) at the finish line. Rocks and trees are stationary. The braves begin at the starting line. The chief turns his back and the braves move from rock to tree quickly and quietly. The chief blows a whistle, turns around, and tries to spot a brave. Braves should be frozen behind a tree or rock, or they are out. The winner is the first brave to cross the finish line.

Intelligence: Intrapersonal   **Curricular Area:** Math

Standard: Understands and applies basic and advanced properties of the concepts of numbers

Benchmark: Understands the relationship among fractions, decimals, mixed numbers, and whole numbers

Size is Relative

Student Activity Sheet

Name: _____ **Date:** _____

Have you ever stood at the bottom of a very tall building and wondered just how tall it was? Think for a moment about the tallest building or the highest mountain you have ever seen. Sometimes it is hard to relate to their massive heights. By comparing a known height (for instance, your height), you will be better able to understand the relationship between the heights of different objects.

How Tall Are You?

A good place to begin your understanding of the height of something is to measure your own height. Work in pairs to measure your heights. Record your height below. Then list your height in inches, feet, centimeters, and meters. For a conversion table, access the following:

- *http://www.mplik.ru/~sg/transl/index.html* (Your browser must be Java capable.)

    Your height in inches: _____

    Your height in feet (use decimals): _____

    Your height in centimeters: _____

    Your height in meters (use decimals): _____

Washington Monument

Let's see how you compare to the Washington Monument. Go to the Web site below and find out the height of the Washington Monument. List its height in inches, feet, centimeters, and meters.

- *http://www.nps.gov/wamo/index2.htm*

    Washington Monument's height in inches: _____

    Washington Monument's height in feet: _____

    Washington Monument's height in centimeters: _____

    Washington Monument's height in meters: _____

Size is Relative *(cont.)*

How Do You Stack Up?

Compare your height to the Washington Monument's height by setting up a ratio in inches, feet, centimeters, and meters. Express your answers as fractions, decimals, and percents. Use the work space at the bottom of the page. Fill in the table with your values.

Inches	Fraction	Decimal	Percent
Your Height ⎯⎯⎯⎯ Washington Monument			

Feet	Fraction	Decimal	Percent
Your Height ⎯⎯⎯⎯ Washington Monument			

Centimeters	Fraction	Decimal	Percent
Your Height ⎯⎯⎯⎯ Washington Monument			

Work Space

Intelligence: Naturalist   **Curricular Area:** Science and Math

Standard: Understands basic concepts about the structure and properties of matter
Benchmark: Knows that properties such as length, weight, temperature, and volume can be measured using appropriate tools
Standard: Understands the nature of scientific inquiry
Benchmark: Plans and conducts simple investigations; uses simple equipment and tools to gather scientific data and extend the senses

Goin' on a Leaf Hunt

You need to find 3 to 5 different types of leaves. They need to be fresh; however, do not pick them off bushes and trees without permission.

In the box, make a rubbing of your favorite leaf. (Your teacher will show you how to do this.)

MY LEAF

My leaf is _____ cm long and _____ cm wide.

The color of my leaf is _____.

The shape of my leaf is _____.

The edge of my leaf is _____.

I can see _____ (number of) veins in my leaf.

My leaf _____ (is/is not) symmetrical.

My leaf is from a _____ tree.

1 2 3 4 5 6 7 8 9 10 11 12 13 14 15

Intelligence: Musical/Rhythmic   **Curricular Area:** Science

Standard: Understands motion and the principles that explain it
Benchmark: Knows that the pitch of a sound depends on the frequency of the vibration producing it

Perfect Pitch

Background

If we talk about making a high sound, which are we referring to—pitch or volume? (pitch) The concept of pitch is something that many children do not understand. Even if they understand that there are different musical notes, they have trouble identifying which ones are higher in pitch. This experiment gives them the opportunity to explore what pitch is.

Objectives

- to understand the concept of pitch
- to make and then test predictions

Background

Explain the difference between volume and pitch. Demonstrate higher and lower volumes, using louder and softer sounds and then demonstrate different pitches. This could be done with a musical instrument such as a piano or recorder, by singing different notes, or by using examples from the animal kingdom. For example, a mouse makes a high-pitched squeak while a lion has a low-pitched roar. Point out that these two animals also have different volumes because a lion's roar is louder than a mouse's squeak.

Materials

- 3 identical 12–16 ounce (350–500 mL) glass bottles
- 1 metal teaspoon (5 mL)
- water
- pitcher
- 1 funnel
- 12" (30 cm) ruler
- bath towel

Directions

Cover the table with a towel. (This helps absorb the spills and keeps the glass bottles from slipping off the table.) Provide a metal teaspoon and three identical bottles (with lids) from juice or soft drinks. Label them A, B, and C. Pour water into each bottle, making sure there are different amounts in each. To minimize spills, put the lids on. If you are going to have students fill the bottles, you will need a funnel and an easy-to-use pitcher.

Follow-Up Activities

Have students predict how the size and shape of a bottle will affect its pitch. Get several bottles and jars of different sizes, and allow students to try them out. Note that there are many variables in this follow-up experiment, so the results are likely to be different from what you would expect. In other words, this is not a controlled experiment. However, this type of follow-up still helps reinforce the basic concepts and motivates students toward doing their own explorations.

Relate the partially filled bottles to a flute, recorder, or clarinet. As you close more of the holes on these instruments, you effectively make the air column longer. This is analogous to taking water out of the bottles to achieve a lower pitch.

Perfect Pitch *(cont.)*

Worksheet—#1

Question

How can I change the pitch of a sound?

Materials

- 3 glass bottles of different sizes
- 1 metal spoon

Directions

Use Bottle A and Bottle B.

1. Tap each bottle with the spoon.

2. Which has a lower pitch?   **Bottle A   Bottle B**

3. Which one has more air?   **Bottle A   Bottle B**

Use Bottle A and Bottle C.

4. Which has more air?   **Bottle A   Bottle C**

5. **Predict:** Which do you think has the lower pitch?   **Bottle A   Bottle C**

6. Tap each bottle with the spoon

7. Which has the lower pitch?   **Bottle A   Bottle C**

Use Bottle B and Bottle C.

8. Which has more air?   **Bottle B   Bottle C**

9. **Predict:** Which do you think has the lower pitch?   **Bottle B   Bottle C**

10. Tap each bottle with the spoon

11. Which has the lower pitch?   **Bottle B   Bottle C**

Conclusion

Does a bottle with more air have a higher or lower pitch? _____

Perfect Pitch

Worksheet—#2

Question

How can I change the pitch of the sound made by tapping a bottle with a spoon?

Materials

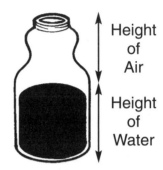

- 3 glass bottles of the same size
- 1 ruler
- water
- 1 metal spoon
- 1 funnel

Directions

1. Use the funnel to fill Bottle A with 1 inch (2.5 cm) of water. Measure how much air is in the bottle: _____ inches (_____ cm).

2. Use the funnel to fill Bottle B with 4 inches (11 cm) of water. Measure how much air is in the bottle: _____ inches (_____ cm).

3. Which bottle has more air in it? **Bottle A**   **Bottle B**

4. Tap each bottle with the spoon.

5. Which bottle has a lower pitch? **Bottle A**   **Bottle B**

6. Now use the funnel to put some water in Bottle C. You choose how much. Measure how much air is in the bottle: _____ inches (_____ cm).

7. Does Bottle C have more or less air than Bottle A? **More Air**   **Less Air**

8. Does Bottle C have more or less air than Bottle B? **More Air**   **Less Air**

9. **Predict:** Do you think Bottle C will have a higher or lower pitch than Bottle A? **Higher**   **Lower**

10. **Predict:** Do you think Bottle C will have a higher or lower pitch than Bottle B? **Higher**   **Lower**

11. Tap each bottle with the spoon.

12. Does Bottle C have a higher or lower pitch than Bottle A? **Higher**   **Lower**

13. Does Bottle C have a higher or lower pitch than Bottle B? **Higher**   **Lower**

Conclusion

Does a bottle with more water have a higher or lower pitch? _____

Intelligence: Logical/Mathematical   **Curricular Area:** Science

Standard: Understands how species depend on one another and on the environment for survival

Benchmark: Knows that an organism's patterns of behavior are related to the nature of that organism's environment

Order

Before beginning your investigation, write your group members' names by their jobs below.

Team Leader _____   Stenographer _____

Biologist_____   Transcriber _____

In the food-chain pyramid below, organize each level according to its particular function or role. Begin by arranging, in order, the list of species provided. Complete the drawing, and label each species in its appropriate placement or level on the food-chain pyramid.

Species Bank

- hawk
- mosquito larvae
- plankton
- minnows
- algae

- turtle
- bass
- worm
- green plant leaves
- spider

- aphid
- duck
- mouse
- lettuce
- humans

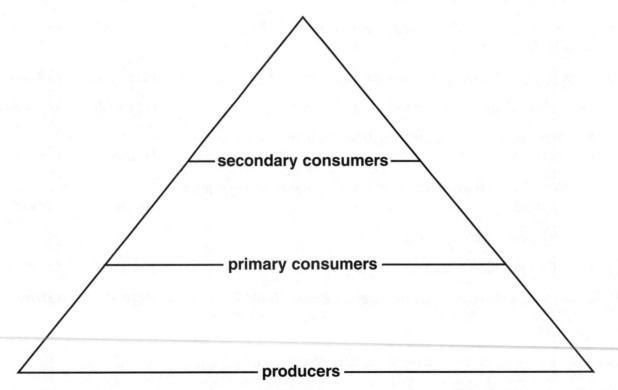

Intelligence: Visual/Spatial   **Curricular Area:** The Arts

Standard: Understands connections among the various art forms and other disciplines

Benchmark: Knows how ideas and emotions are expressed in the various art forms

Standard: Understands and applies media, techniques, and processes related to the visual arts

Benchmark: Knows the differences among visual characteristics and purposes

Rhapsody in Color

One of George Gershwin's most famous compositions is "Rhapsody in Blue." Create your own "Rhapsody in Color" with the illustration on this page. Use only one color and its various tints and shades to complete the picture. Share your creative "rhapsody" with the class.

Rhapsody in _____

Intelligence: Interpersonal   **Curricular Area:** The Arts

Standard: Understands choreographic principles, processes, and structures
Benchmark: Uses partner skills such as copying, leading and following, and mirroring
Standard: Understands dance in various cultures and historical periods
Benchmark: Knows folk dances from various cultures

Folk Dancing

Here are some simple folk dances your students will enjoy learning.

Latin American Rumba

Use lively Latin American folk music that has a fast beat. The directions below indicate which way the boys should move. The girls' movements should mirror the boys'. If students have difficulty coordinating their dance steps with a partner, have them try the dance by themselves.

Directions

Step 1:   Assign a partner for each student. If possible, have each girl paired with a boy. If this is not possible, assign one student to play the part of the girl and the other student to play the part of the boy.

Step 2:   Have the partners stand facing each other. Have the boys step forward with their left feet and push their weight onto them.

Step 3:   Have the boys step to the right with their right feet and push their weight onto them.

Step 4:   Have the boys move their left feet close to their right feet. Have them push their weight onto their left feet.

Step 5:   Have the boys step back with their right feet and push their weight onto them.

Step 6:   Have the boys step to the left with their left feet and push their weight onto them.

Step 7:   Have the boys move their right feet close to their left feet. Have them push their weight onto the right feet. Then have students repeat steps 2–7.

Greek Hapapikos

Use fast Greek music.

Directions

Step 1:   Have students form a circle with their hands on one another's shoulders. Have them move their right feet one step to the right side.

Step 2:   Have students cross their left feet over their right feet.

Step 3:   Have them move their right feet one step to the right.

Step 4:   Have students hop on their right feet.

Step 5:   Have students move their left feet one step to the left.

Step 6:   Have them hop on their left feet. Have students repeat steps 2–6.

Assigned-Task Assessment: The 3 P's

The 3 P's of assessment are Portfolios, Performances, and Projects. Any one of these forms can be used to document and assess student achievement of benchmarks and standards.

1. Portfolios

Portfolios form a general and multi-dimensional background for assessment methods. More ways to use them are listed on pages 106–112.

2. Performances

As is true with the term "portfolio," performance assessment is a general, multiple-meaning term. It covers writing assessments and some open-ended math assessments in which the end product of the student's performance is rated or scored. In these examples, the assessment is considered performance assessment because the student has generated the product which can then be scored with a rubric. Performance assessment can also be the actual observation of the student in action. This process of observation might consist of watching a student do a science experiment or participate in a cooperative learning group. This kind of performance assessment can be documented with a checklist. (See pages 113–121.)

3. Projects

Projects qualify as a kind of performance assessment in two ways: they are generated by the student, and they take long enough to allow for observing the student in action. They can be documented in many ways. The observer can use a checklist. The activities can be photographed and/or filmed with a video camera. Any oral component can be taped. All of the pieces—the evidence, so to speak—can be collected and stored in a portfolio. Projects are often associated with social studies; however they can be used in any area of the curriculum. (See pages 122–127.)

Note: Both **performances** and **projects** are good examples of assessments that are trying to be authentic. The assigned tasks that prompt these two kinds of assessment should come as close as possible to "real life" activities. They should possess the characteristics that identify them as alternative assessments: They should be complex (involving a group of learning behaviors), open-ended (permitting more than one solution), and coherent (resulting in a single product).

Portfolios

In the past few years, many definitions have been assigned to the term *portfolio* with respect to assessment in the classroom. Perhaps the most meaningful definition for portfolio might also be the simplest. A portfolio is a collection of student work samples that can give a clearer picture of that student's progress and achievements than many traditional methods of assessment can.

There are also as many different types of portfolios as there are subjects in the curriculum. They may come in the form of shoe boxes, file folders, spiral notebooks, videotapes, or cassette tapes. A portfolio can include tests, work samples, projects, anecdotal records, and self-evaluation checklists. Most educators agree that portfolios are more than assessment tools because they provide an in-depth look at the actual accomplishments and progress of individual students. For this reason, too, they can be excellent tools for looking at student achievement of standards.

Initially, it seemed as though primary teachers were the first to embrace the idea of portfolio assessment, probably because many of them had already been using portfolios in their classrooms for years. Reading and writing were probably two of the most popular subjects for which students and teachers constructed portfolios. Now, teachers in all areas of the curriculum and across all grade levels are gaining valuable assessment information from the use of portfolios.

The subject of a thematic unit is an excellent opportunity to incorporate the use of portfolios to assess standards. For example, students can assemble a portfolio based on a unit of study of immigrants. Benchmarks which will need to be addressed in the portfolio include the following:

- Knows the various movements of large groups of people in the history of the U.S.
- Understands the experience of immigrant groups
- Knows the reasons why various groups migrated to different parts of the U.S.

Knowing in advance the standards and benchmarks which will need to be met, students can select work samples, tests, projects, or other activities to include in their portfolio.

Portfolios that provide the most effective way of assessing students usually contain the following key elements:

1. A portfolio cover designed by the student.
2. A table of contents showing the following for each piece of work: the title, the date it was completed, a brief comment explaining why it was chosen, and the page number to tell where it appears in the portfolio.
3. The contents—work samples, projects, etc. These should be organized according to the table of contents.
4. Evaluation forms should include a self-evaluation completed by the student and the evaluations completed by people who review the portfolio, such as teachers, parents, administrators, and other visitors. These evaluations may be (a) checklists which are simple to complete and do not take much time, (b) sentence starters to be completed with short responses which provide some structure, or (c) letters which allow for open-ended remarks.

Portfolio Directions

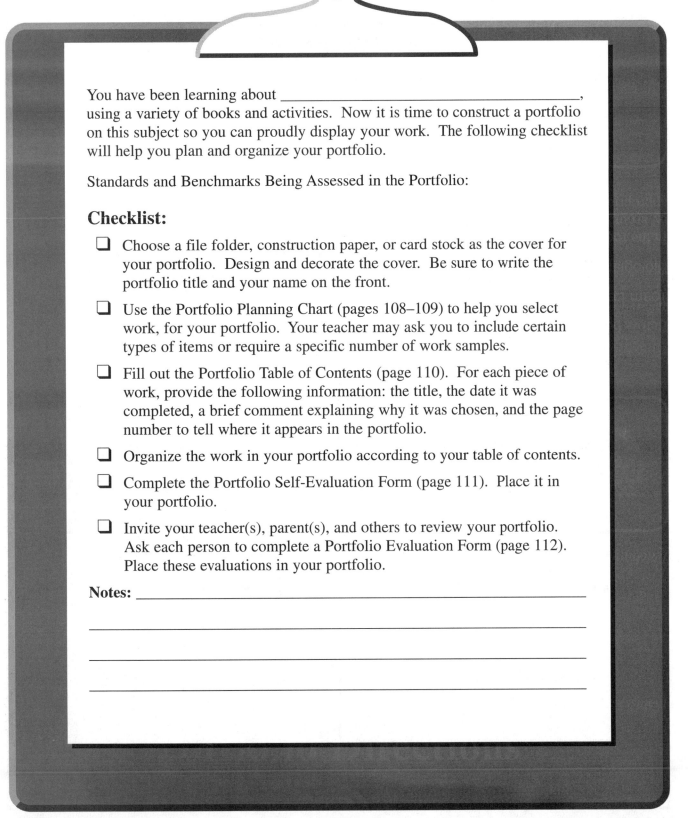

You have been learning about _____,
using a variety of books and activities. Now it is time to construct a portfolio
on this subject so you can proudly display your work. The following checklist
will help you plan and organize your portfolio.

Standards and Benchmarks Being Assessed in the Portfolio:

Checklist:

❑ Choose a file folder, construction paper, or card stock as the cover for
your portfolio. Design and decorate the cover. Be sure to write the
portfolio title and your name on the front.

❑ Use the Portfolio Planning Chart (pages 108–109) to help you select
work, for your portfolio. Your teacher may ask you to include certain
types of items or require a specific number of work samples.

❑ Fill out the Portfolio Table of Contents (page 110). For each piece of
work, provide the following information: the title, the date it was
completed, a brief comment explaining why it was chosen, and the page
number to tell where it appears in the portfolio.

❑ Organize the work in your portfolio according to your table of contents.

❑ Complete the Portfolio Self-Evaluation Form (page 111). Place it in
your portfolio.

❑ Invite your teacher(s), parent(s), and others to review your portfolio.
Ask each person to complete a Portfolio Evaluation Form (page 112).
Place these evaluations in your portfolio.

Notes: _____

_____

_____

_____

Portfolio Planning Chart

Below is an example of a Portfolio Planning Chart which may be used to assemble a portfolio in social studies on immigrants. Use the blank chart on page 109 to develop your own Portfolio Planning Chart to go with a unit you have been studying.

Reading and Language Arts

Venn Diagram of three immigration stories

Family History

Survival Guide

Social Studies	**Geography**
Who? When? Why?—Chart of the Immigrant Experience	Immigrant Mapping Activity
Ancestor Doll and Writing Description	Where Is Your Family From?
Parent Questionnaire	

Art	**Math/Free Choice Activities**
Arrival View Diorama	Graph the Immigrants
	Math of the Statue of Liberty

Portfolio Planning Chart

Portfolio Table of Contents

Selected Work	Date Completed	Why I Chose It	Page Number

Portfolio Self-Evaluation Form

1. Three things I learned about _____ were _____
_____ .

2. The most interesting item in this portfolio is_____
because _____ .

3. In studying about _____, the part that I enjoyed the most
was _____ .

4. Something about _____ I do not understand
is _____

5. The book I most enjoyed reading was _____

6. I designed the cover of my portfolio this way because _____
_____

7. When people look at my portfolio, I want them to pay special attention to _____
_____

8. Three people I would especially like to view my portfolio are _____
_____

9. Here are some suggestions for my next portfolio project: _____
_____
_____

Signature: _____ **Date:** _____

Portfolio Evaluation Form

You have been asked to review this student's portfolio related to his or her studies of the topic assigned. Please take time to look through this student's work and accomplishments. Use the space below to write this student a letter which gives your reactions to the portfolio. You may note any projects that particularly interested or impressed you. You may wish to include your own reflections about his or her topic or tell about similar activities you recall doing when you were in school. Please remember to date and sign your letter.

_____
         Date

Dear _____ ,

_____

_____

_____

_____

_____

_____

_____

_____

_____

Sincerely,

_____

Performance Tasks

Performance assessment is a means to evaluate students in a variety of contexts. It allows them to demonstrate their understanding of concepts and to apply knowledge and skills they have acquired. Performance assessment tasks are carefully constructed in order to assess specific declarative and procedural knowledge and critical thinking skills, as well as to determine student achievement of standards and benchmarks. Declarative knowledge refers to facts about certain persons, places, and things, and also encompasses generalizations or concepts that can be derived based on those facts. Procedural knowledge refers to skills and strategies. The tasks used to assess this knowledge are scored based on grading rubrics that are, in most cases, established by the teacher prior to introducing the task.

A rubric is a set of criteria students see prior to engaging in the performance task. The rubric identifies the qualities the teacher expects to see in responses at several points along a scale. By viewing established criteria prior to the activity, students clearly know what is expected in order to receive a specific score. Each score on the rubric is matched to an example of a response.

A rubric can be used in two ways: as an assessment tool and as a teaching tool. When a rubric is used as an *assessment* tool, it serves as a standard against which samples of students' work can be measured. When a rubric is used as a *teaching* tool, it provides an example for students to follow and can actually promote learning by offering clear performance standards for students.

How to Use Performance Assessments and Rubrics

The construction of a performance task can be a time-consuming process. With practice, however, the tasks become easier to write. An added benefit is that the tasks can be used from one year to the next so you will not have to recreate a whole new set of tasks each school year.

The first step in creating a performance task is to determine what standard you wish to assess. Then you should determine if this standard is declarative or procedural. If you are assessing declarative knowledge, your task should require students to respond in some fashion to a generalization. Students will then respond to this generalization according to the task, using their knowledge of basic facts. If you are assessing procedural knowledge, students will be required to apply a strategy such as a problem-solving strategy. In their application of this strategy, they must naturally apply their knowledge of basic skills. You must also consider what critical thinking skills students will have to use in order to complete the performance tasks.

Performance Tasks *(cont.)*

Next, you must determine the type of performance task you will use to assess the declarative or procedural knowledge. Examples of 11 types of performance assessment tasks are explained on page 115. Once you have made all of the important decisions about what you want to assess, you can write the task. Like any other piece of writing, it may take several drafts before you are completely satisfied. In the task, you should include the ways in which the students will present their findings or answers. Some presentation ideas may include a written report, a letter to an official, or an oral report. See pages 116–118 for an example of a performance task. Pages 119–121 will help you create your own performance task.

Once you have completed writing the task, you must develop a rubric to score student responses. You may wish to have about two to three categories of performance standards on your rubric.

The task and the rubric should be established and discussed clearly with students prior to the activity. Keep in mind that the burden of establishing criteria does not always have to rest upon the teacher. Students' opinions can be solicited prior to establishing the rubric; even first graders can participate in this process. By assisting in the creation of a rubric, students may become more aware of task expectations and therefore, they may perform better. Of course, it is up to the teacher to ensure that the rubric matches the performance task and measures the intended standard(s). An example of a rubric written for a specific performance task is on page 118. See pages 141–144 for more information on creating your own rubric.

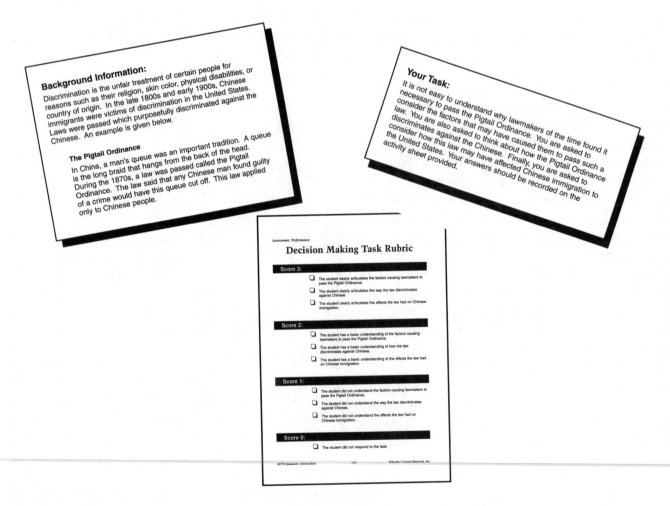

Performance Task Types and Descriptions

Comparison Task: The student is required to compare two or more people, places, or things.

Classification Task: The student is asked to classify, or put into categories, certain people, places, or things.

Position Support Task: The student is asked to take a position on a subject or issue and defend that position.

Application Task: The student is asked to apply his or her knowledge in a new situation.

Analyzing Perspectives Task: The student is asked to analyze two to three different perspectives and then choose the perspective he or she supports.

Decision-Making Task: The student must identify the factors that caused a certain decision to be made.

Historical Perspective Task: The student must consider differing theories to answer historical questions.

Predictive Task: The student must make predictions about what could have happened or will happen in the future.

Problem-Solving Task: The student must create a solution to a specific problem.

Invention Task: The student must create something new and unique.

Error Identification Task: The student must identify specific errors or misrepresentations.

Sample of a Decision-Making Task

Background Information:

Discrimination is the unfair treatment of certain people for reasons such as their religion, skin color, physical disabilities, or country of origin. In the late 1800s and early 1900s, Chinese immigrants were victims of discrimination in the United States. Laws were passed which purposefully discriminated against the Chinese. An example is given below.

The Pigtail Ordinance

In China, a man's queue was an important tradition. A queue is the long braid that hangs from the back of the head. During the 1870s, a law was passed called the Pigtail Ordinance. The law said that any Chinese man found guilty of a crime would have this queue cut off. This law applied only to Chinese people.

Your Task:

It is not easy to understand why lawmakers of the time found it necessary to pass the Pigtail Ordinance. You are asked to consider the factors that may have caused them to pass such a law. You are also asked to think about how the Pigtail Ordinance discriminates against the Chinese. Finally, you are asked to consider how this law may have affected Chinese immigration to the United States. Your answers should be recorded on the activity sheet provided.

Decision-Making
Task Activity Sheet

Name

Date

1. List the factors that you think may have caused lawmakers to pass the Pigtail Ordinance.

_____

_____

_____

_____

2. In what ways does the Pigtail Ordinance discriminate against the Chinese?

_____

_____

_____

_____

3. What effects could the Pigtail Ordinance have had on Chinese immigration?

_____

_____

_____

_____

Decision-Making Task Rubric

Score 3:

❑ The student clearly articulates the factors causing lawmakers to pass the Pigtail Ordinance.

❑ The student clearly articulates the way the law discriminates against the Chinese.

❑ The student clearly articulates the effects the law had on Chinese immigration.

Score 2:

❑ The student has a basic understanding of the factors causing lawmakers to pass the Pigtail Ordinance.

❑ The student has a basic understanding of how the law discriminates against the Chinese.

❑ The student has a basic understanding of the effects the law had on Chinese immigration.

Score 1:

❑ The student did not understand the factors causing lawmakers to pass the Pigtail Ordinance.

❑ The student did not understand the way the law discriminates against the Chinese.

❑ The student did not understand the effects the law had on Chinese immigration.

Score 0:

❑ The student did not respond to the task.

Selecting a Task— Questions to Ask Yourself

Use these questions to help you decide on a task to prompt your performance assessment. Add more if you wish.

Task Being Considered _____

Questions to Ask

1. Does this task match any standards? Which ones?

   _____

   _____

   _____

2. Will the completed task reflect the skills and knowledge my students should acquire? What are they?

   _____

   _____

   _____

   _____

3. Are several disciplines represented in the task? Which ones?

   _____

   _____

   _____

4. Will the task measure more than one standard? If so, what are they?

   _____

   _____

   _____

Describing the Task—
Questions to Ask Yourself

Use these questions to help you describe the task you choose. Add other questions that are relevant or important to you.

Task Being Considered _____

Questions to Ask

1. How will the questions to the students be asked? Give examples.

   _____

   _____

   _____

   _____

2. Will the work be done individually, in groups, or as a combination of both? Describe.

   _____

   _____

   _____

   _____

3. What materials will I need? List.

   _____

   _____

   _____

   _____

4. How much time will be allowed? Will all of the work be done at school, or will homework be assigned?

   _____

   _____

   _____

Setting Scoring Criteria—Questions to Ask Yourself

Use these questions to help you decide on scoring criteria. Add others that are important to you.

Task Being Considered _____

Questions to Ask

1. How will I know that students have made an excellent response? an acceptable response? a poor response?

   _____

   _____

   _____

   _____

2. Do I have models of responses that reflect various skill levels?

   _____

   _____

   _____

   _____

3. How does completion of this task relate to my instructional goals?

   _____

   _____

   _____

   _____

4. How does completion of this task relate to the standards?

   _____

   _____

   _____

   _____

Research Projects

Research projects provide yet another opportunity to assess student understanding of standards and benchmarks. Projects are similar to a performance task; however, usually an extended period of time is given to complete the project. Additionally, each student can potentially choose a different project to demonstrate competence of a standard or benchmark. The key to using projects successfully for assessment is to be sure that students have an understanding of what they will need to demonstrate with the final project.

There may be times you wish to assess a standard or benchmark, using a project in which you would like all of your students to work on the same project. In this case, a description of the standard students will be addressing and a description of the project should be provided for students. (See pages 124 and 125 for examples.) Other times, you may wish to give students the standard or benchmark and allow them to choose a project which would demonstrate their understanding of the standard or benchmark. (See page 126 for an example.)

How to Use Research Projects

Probably the most difficult skill for students to master when doing long-term projects is time management. The Independent Research Contract is included on page 123. This contract can help students better manage their time for the project.

It will also be necessary to train students on oral presentation skills. You may need to model appropriate public speaking skills by making a formal presentation to the class yourself.

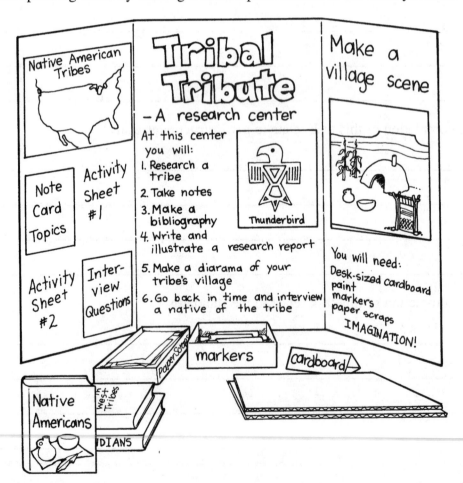

Independent Research Contract

Name _____ Date _____

The Project:

My research topic is _____

What do I need to know? _____

Where will I get this information? _____

Time Line: (Provide dates.)

I will begin my research _____

I will present a progress report _____

I will conclude my study _____

I will present my final report _____

Presentation:

_____ I will present my research in a paper.

_____ I will do an oral presentation of my research to the class.

_____ I will make a physical project to present my research (diorama, poster, etc.).

Standard: Understands the history of a local community and how communities in North America varied long ago
Benchmark: Knows geographical settings, economic activities, food, clothing, homes, crafts, and rituals of Native American societies long ago

Diorama of a Tribal Scene

(*Sample Project*)

After completing a unit on Native Americans, students could be assigned a project to design a diorama of a tribal scene.

Materials

- 1 desk-sized piece of cardboard
- paper scraps
- markers or crayons
- dirt or sand
- leaves and twigs
- information

Directions

Choose one of the tribes studied in class and create a tribal scene diorama. Use the questions and statements below to help guide your project.

1. Using the desk-sized piece of cardboard, make the environment of your tribe. Did they live in the forest, the desert, or near the ocean? Use dirt, sand, leaves, and twigs to create the land for the tribe.

2. Create the tribal homes. Did they live in large groups? small groups? single dwellings? Did they live in a tipi? a hogan? a longhouse?

3. Make men, women, and children of the tribe. Add them to your diorama. How did they dress? What activities did they do? Display them doing those activities.

4. Did your tribe farm? hunt? herd animals? Be sure your display shows this.

5. What type of cooking utensils did your tribe use? Did they make baskets? Did they make pottery? Have them in your display.

6. What type of weapons did your tribe use? Add them to your diorama.

7. In what religious rituals and ceremonies did the tribe participate?

8. Think of what else would have been included in a village scene.

Standard: Uses basic and advanced procedures while performing the processes of computation
Benchmarks: Adds, subtracts, multiplies, and divides whole numbers and decimals; solves real-world problems

The Pet Shop

Have you ever had a mouse, rat, or hamster for a pet? Rodents can make great pets and provide a lot of pleasure to their owners.

Activity

If you have ever had a pet, you know there are many responsibilities involved. Pets need to be cared for, fed, cleaned, exercised, and loved on a regular basis. Having a pet is very much like being a parent. For this activity, you will pretend to buy a pet mouse. Your job is to research and purchase all the necessary equipment, food, toys, and whatever else is needed to make your mouse happy and healthy. You will be given a budget of $50.00, so be sure to stay within that budget. After you have set up your pet mouse's home, write a quick reference guide about your new mouse. Maybe you could call this helpful book "Important Mice Advice." This will be a mini-book which provides important tips on handling and caring for mice.

A good way to find information on mouse care is to visit a local pet store. If you decide to do this, be sure to call the owner or manager first to make an appointment. By doing this, you will be assured of reserving some special time with the owner, as well as respecting his/her busy schedule. Another source to use is the library. There are many books about mice and ideas on how to keep one as a pet.

Below is a partial listing of some significant facts for pet mouse care.

- A standard 10-gallon glass aquarium makes a nice home for mice. Small aquariums are inexpensive and easy to keep clean.
- The foods most commonly eaten by mice are seeds, lettuce, and carrots. Mice cannot eat many of the foods that humans enjoy eating.
- Mice are very social creatures and live in colonies in the wild. It is best to have two mice for their social happiness and health. A good combination is two females. Two males will constantly fight. A female and male is also a good combination, but you may end up with more mice than you bargained for.
- Buying the mouse is the last step. Always buy your mouse from a clean pet store that takes good care of its animals. Choose animals that are lively, slender, and alert. Their eyes should be wide open. Do not buy a mouse that wheezes or coughs.

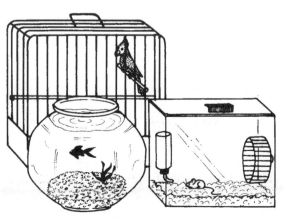

For your project, create a tally of your "expenses" and try to stay within your budget. Give your pretend pet mouse a name, and draw an illustration of your pet in its new home. For your "Mice Advice" book, jot down any ideas or suggestions that you have found.

Standard: Demonstrates competence in the general skills and strategies for reading a variety of literary texts
Benchmark: Identifies setting, main characters, main events, and problems in the stories
Standard: Demonstrates competence in the general skills and strategies of the writing process
Benchmark: Writes in response to literature; writes in a variety of formats

Book Report Ideas

There are so many different ways to do a book report. After you finish reading *The Mouse and the Motorcycle* by Beverly Cleary (Avon, 1965), choose one of the following projects that interests you. If you have an idea of your own, ask your teacher if you may do that instead. Have fun and be creative!

Pen Pal

Write a letter to one of the characters in *The Mouse and the Motorcycle*. Tell him/her how your life is like and unlike his/hers. Ask that character questions and offer your opinions about some of the situations in the story. Then, write a letter back to yourself, pretending to be that character.

Talk-Show Host

Pretend that you are a television talk-show host and will be interviewing a character from *The Mouse and the Motorcycle*. Compose a list of questions in which your viewers would be interested. Ask one of your friends to be the character, and then conduct a "live taping" of your show or produce a video.

Movie Marquee

The Mouse and the Motorcycle is about to become a major movie, and you have been chosen to design the promotional poster. Include the title, author of the book, a listing of the major characters in the book and the actors and actresses who will play them, and a short paragraph summarizing the story.

Mobile Magic

Create and assemble an exciting and colorful mobile to display in your classroom. Using a coat hanger, string or fishing wire and heavy paper, show the plot, setting, and characters of *The Mouse and the Motorcycle*. Start by placing the setting at the top level, the characters at the middle level, and the plot development at the bottom level.

Mystery Box Game

Cover a shoe box with construction paper and color large question marks all over the box. On one side of the box, write the title of the book. Fill your box with five objects that are related to *The Mouse and the Motorcycle*. (Examples could be an aspirin, a toy motorcycle or car, etc.) Allow the class time to ask "yes" or "no" questions about the objects. When someone correctly guesses the object, he/she will need to explain how the object relates to the story.

Patchwork Quilt

Use a piece of 18" x 26" (45 cm x 65 cm) tagboard and six 8" x 8" (20 cm x 20 cm) squares of paper. Glue the squares on the tagboard and simulate stitching around each piece, using a crayon or marker. Then, have each of the squares tell specific information about *The Mouse and the Motorcycle*. One square should state the title and author, and the other squares should tell about the characters, plot, and settings.

Project Evaluation: Individual Students

Name:_____

Research Project:_____

Standard(s) Being Assessed:_____

1 = poor   2 = average   3 = good   4 = excellent

Skill	Score			
	1	**2**	**3**	**4**
Student demonstrates an understanding of the standard(s) being assessed:				
Examples:				
Project meets requirements				
Examples:				
Extras included (cover, pictures)				
Examples:				
Oral report given to class				
Comments:				
Extra-credit work				
Examples:				

Documentation of Student Achievement

Checklists

Checklists are important because they go with many kinds of assessments. They document performances and projects. They fit right into portfolios. Checklists are used for two main reasons: to keep a running list of what has been accomplished by a student and to document standards and benchmarks that are behavior based. Checklists can be useful to give an overall picture of what a student is capable of and areas in which the student still needs to grow. Additionally, checklists can also be useful for documenting standards and benchmarks which tend not to leave a "paper trail." Benchmarks such as "Understands how print is organized and read (left to right, top to bottom)" are easily documented on a checklist by teacher observation. Both samples of checklists and blank checklists for you to use are provided on pages 130–133.

Anecdotal Records and Observations

Anecdotal records are simply teacher notes based on observations in the classroom. Students should be "watched" or observed in a variety of settings and activities. Observe them during instructional time, free time, working by themselves, with partners or in small groups, and with best friends. Observe students anywhere and anytime you can! As you observe students, use anecdotal records to indicate what you saw at that time. Teacher Data Capture sheets can also be designed for noting observations for a specific task. Pages 134–140 provide various methods and forms for recording your observations.

Rubrics

The word "rubric" literally means "rule." When the word is used in connection with assessment, a rubric is a scoring guide that differentiates, on an articulated scale, a range from the excellent response to the one that is inappropriate and needs revision. A personal rubric workshop is provided on pages 141–144. Uses these pages to help you design your own rubrics.

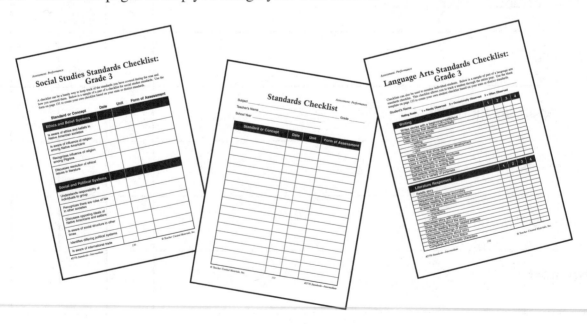

Checklists

So What Are Checklists?

At first mention, checklists sound easy and self explanatory. They are, of course, lists of things to be checked off by the observer in the course of observing a performance. But what things? That is the important and very controversial question.

We have gotten into the habit of depending on objective, multiple-choice tests designed to measure incremental and usually minimal proficiency skills to tell us what our students know. For instance, many reading tests measure knowledge of phonics. A good reader—someone who can read words and comprehend their meaning—who learned to read by generalizing from a sight vocabulary might not necessarily do well on a phonics test.

And How Do We Make a Checklist?

So how do we make our checklists? We do what is called a task analysis. We figure out what really goes into the achievement of a particular standard or benchmark. In the case of a reading test, we would have to define what we meant by *reading*. Hard as that might be, it is easy compared to deciding what we mean by *knowing* or *understanding* or *using science*, for example.

We will have to remember that performance is knowledge in use. We must look for evidence that knowledge has been acquired and then look at the competence and originality with which that knowledge is applied to the given problem. We must leave out things that do not really support the evidence for which we are looking and put in the things that are important.

Another approach to the checklist is to simply take a district or state standards list and use it. You may need to add some criteria to tell you how you will recognize that the content is there and how well it has been achieved. After charting the standards and benchmarks, you can begin observing students for evidence of an understanding of the standard.

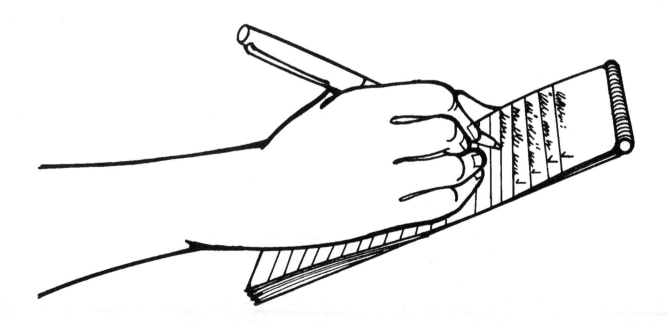

Social Studies Checklist: Grade 3

A checklist can be a handy way to keep track of the benchmarks you have covered during the year and how you assessed them. Below is a sample of part of a checklist for social studies benchmarks. Use the form on page 131 to create your own checklist based on your state or district standards and benchmarks.

Standard or Concept	Date	Unit	Form of Assessment
Ethics and Belief Systems			
Is aware of ethics and beliefs in Native American societies			
Is aware of the influence of religion among Native Americans			
Recognizes the influence of religion among Pilgrims			
Discusses resolution of ethical issues in literature			
Social and Political Systems			
Understands responsibility of individuals to group			
Recognizes there are rules of law in other societies			
Discusses opposing ideals of Native Americans and settlers			
Is aware of social structure in other times			
Identifies differing political systems			
Is aware of international trade			

Checklist

Subject _____ Grade _____

Teacher's Name _____

School Year _____

Standard or Concept	Date	Unit	Form of Assessment

Language Arts Checklist: Grade 3

Checklists can also be used to monitor individual students. Below is a sample of part of a language arts checklist. This checklist allows you to track a student through the entire year. Use the blank template on page 133 to create your own student checklist based on your state or district standards and benchmarks.

Student's Name _____

Rating Scale: 1 = Rarely Observed   2 = Occasionally Observed   3 = Often Observed

Writing	1	2	3
Writes stories with a beginning/middle/end			
Writes stories that develop sequentially			
Uses descriptive words			
Uses story elements:			
—setting			
—character			
—plot			
Writes stories that show character development			
Uses a variety of vocabulary			
Uses a variety of sentence structures			
Engages promptly in writing task			
Sustains attention to writing task			
Self-selects writing topics			
Writes for a variety of purposes			

Literature Responses	1	2	3
Retells story			
Summarizes story			
Sequences story events accurately			
Relates reading to personal experience			
Is aware of story elements:			
—setting			
—characters			
—plot			
Discusses story with others			
Gives opinions about the story			
Extends reading through related projects			
Discusses meanings of stories			
Draws conclusions about story			
Distinguishes fact from fiction			
Compares and contrasts characters			

Standards Checklist

Subject _____ Grade _____

Students's Name _____

Rating Scale: **1 = Rarely Observed**   **2 = Occasionally Observed**   **3 = Often Observed**

Standards	1	2	3

Anecdotal Records and Observations

Anecdotal notes and observations are carefully documented records of certain events, behaviors, and skills. They provide records that you can review independently or share with parents during conference time. When these notes and observations are put together, they tell an ongoing story about the student's growth and progress.

Anecdotal records and observations can be objective or interpretive. When using the objective style, you simply record what you are seeing as if you were a camera. If you wish to go beyond merely recording, you can try the interpretive style in which you would actually evaluate and comment on your notes and observations. This may be helpful to assist you in recognizing the implications of your observations.

Some teachers make a commitment to formally observe each student every few weeks. Others may choose to formally observe a student once a month or once during a single grading period. Your choice will ultimately depend on your available time and class size.

At the beginning of the year, it may be necessary to make more general entries as you begin the process of becoming familiar with your students. As you get to know your students throughout the school year, your entries may become more specific, or the types of entries may change. For instance, at the beginning of the year you may make general notes about students. As the year progresses, your notes may become more specific and detailed, focusing more on standards and observations based on student performance.

There are several ways to record anecdotal records and observations. Examples of forms and blank templates are provided for you on pages 135–138. Use whichever type of form with which you feel most comfortable.

A teacher may wish to create a Teacher Data Capture sheet for documenting observations of a specific task. The purpose of the Teacher Data Capture sheet is to replace that which the teacher has mentally filed. The information recorded on the sheet provides documentation for the task. Key words such as "displayed," "modeled," "exhibited," and "demonstrated" usually appear first in the phrases for quick references, and boxes are provided for handy check-off. For example, if you are going to observe each student in your classroom using skip counting to count coins, you may wish to create a form which will focus your attention on specific aspects of that task. (See the Teacher Data Capture Sheet on pages 139–140 for an example.)

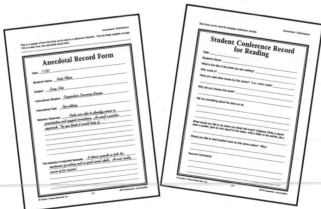

This is a sample of how this form can be used in a classroom situation. Use the blank template on page 136 to create your own anecdotal record form.

Anecdotal Record Form

Date: *11/20*

Student's Name: *Paolo Albero*

Subject: *Lang. Arts*

Instructional Situation: *Cooperative Learning Groups*

Instructional Task: *Peer editing*

Behavior Observed: *Paolo was able to identify errors in punctuation and suggest corrections. He used a positive approach: "Do you think it would help if..."*

This behavior is important because . . . *it shows growth in both the mechanics of writing and in good social skills. He was really aware of his success!*

This is a blank copy of the same form that was demonstrated on page 135. It can be duplicated and used for keeping your own anecdotal records.

Anecdotal Record Form

Date: _____

Student's Name: _____

Subject: _____

Instructional Situation: _____

Instructional Task: _____

Behavior Observed: _____

_____

_____

_____

_____

_____

_____

_____

This behavior is important because: . . . _____

_____

_____

_____

_____

This form can be used for keeping conference records.

Student Conference Record for Reading

Date: _____

Student's Name: _____

What is the title of the book you are reading? _____

Who wrote it? _____

Have you read other books by this author? If so, which ones?_____

_____

Why did you choose this book? _____

_____

Tell me something about the story so far.

_____

_____

_____

What would you like to do when you finish this book? (Options: Write a report, draw a poster, give an oral report to the class, write a letter to the author, etc.)

_____

Would you like to read another book by this same author? Why?

_____

_____

Teacher Comments:

_____

_____

_____

This form can be used for keeping conference records.

- -

Student Conference Record
for Writing

Date: _____

Student's Name: _____

What is the title of the piece on which you are now working?

_____

What kind of piece is it? (story, poem, essay, report, etc.)

_____

How far have you gotten in the writing process? (rough draft, self-editing, peer editing, polishing)

_____

What do you plan to do next with this piece?

_____

_____

What do you like best about this piece?

_____

_____

Is there anything you would like to change on this piece?

_____

_____

Teacher Comments: _____

_____

_____

_____

Teacher Data Capture Sheet

(sample)

This type of Teacher Data Capture Sheet can be used to focus your attention on specific aspects of a performance task. This Teacher Data Capture Sheet was designed to go with a performance task asking students to show various fractions and decimals, using fraction bars. Use the blank template on page 140 to create your own data capture sheet based on your state or district standards or benchmarks based on your performance task.

Y = Yes, behavior exhibited; **S** = behavior somewhat exhibited; **N** = behavior not exhibited

Student's Name _____ Date _____

	Y	S	N	
1.	❑	❑	❑	. . . displayed an adequate understanding of the task at hand.
2.	❑	❑	❑	. . . contributed to group discussion on activity.
3.	❑	❑	❑	. . . displayed knowledge of the term "equal" relative to fraction bars.
4.	❑	❑	❑	. . . displayed an understanding of less than one.
5.	❑	❑	❑	. . . modeled appropriate use of the fraction bars for activity.
6.	❑	❑	❑	. . . reviewed his/her work.

Overall, the student's performance *[circle choice below]* **expectations.**

went beyond   *met overall*   *met partial*   *met minimal*   *did not meet*

Notes: _____

_____

_____

_____

_____

_____

_____

_____

Teacher Data Capture Sheet

(template)

Y = Yes, behavior exhibited; **S** = behavior somewhat exhibited; **N** = behavior not exhibited

Student's Name _____ Date _____

	Y	**S**	**N**
1.	☐	☐	☐	_____
2.	☐	☐	☐	_____
3.	☐	☐	☐	_____
4.	☐	☐	☐	_____
5.	☐	☐	☐	_____
6.	☐	☐	☐	_____

Overall, the student's performance *[circle choice]* **expectations.**

went beyond　　　*met overall*　　　*met partial*　　　*met minimal*　　　*did not meet*

Notes: _____

_____

_____

_____

_____

_____

_____

Do-It-Yourself Directions: A Personal Rubric Workshop

How Do I Begin?

First of all, it is important to know that your prompt or task and your rubric are part of the same package. Secondly, it is vital to realize that this is an interactive procedure—you will write, try out, and revise your prompt/rubric package until it tells you what you really want to know. Getting it exactly right the first time is a result of years of experience or plain luck!

Write the Rubric First

It is probably easier to write the rubric first. A three-point rubric is the easiest, and you can begin at any point. The three points of a three-point rubric parallel one another and reflect different levels of the same skills. The "High Pass" contains all of the features of the "Pass" either in identical form or as a more advanced variation. "Needs Revision" considers parallel features, but they may be expressed as negatives.

Decide what you will be assessing in your rubric. Once you have decided what to include in your rubric, it must appear in some form in all of the points.

Write the Prompt

Your prompt should be written to elicit a response that will allow assessment of the points in your rubric. If your "High Pass" requires the students to write more than one complete sentence, you should not instruct them to write "a sentence." This seems really obvious, but sometimes you will not catch this kind of thing until you are reading a batch of papers. If you suddenly realize that you are not getting any high papers, you may want to look back at the wording of your prompt.

Revise, Revise, Revise

There are many reasons to consider revising your rubric and/or prompt. Look for some of these:

1. No high papers
   —Did I require something I have not taught?
   —Did I require something in the rubric for which I did not ask in the prompt?
2. All high papers
   —Did I want this result? (It is possible for everyone to do really well.)
3. No passing papers
   —Were the directions wrong or easy to misinterpret?
   —Was the format different from our usual assignments?
4. Results inconsistent with the way I see my class
   —Do I need to look at the prompt/rubric package?
   —Do I need to take another look at the class?

Rubrics are Power

Feeling comfortable with rubric writing gives you a powerful position in the assessment process. You will always be able to justify your results and demonstrate how you obtained them.

Do-It-Yourself Teacher Script

Use this blank form to create your own teacher script for a writing sample prompt.

Prompt for a Writing Sample

Teacher Script

Teacher Says:

Today you are going to show me how well you can write.

Read to yourself as I read aloud.

Writing Situation: _____

_____

_____

_____

_____

Directions for Writing: _____

_____

_____

_____

_____

You may start.

(Pause. Repeat "Writing Situation" and "Directions for Writing" as may be necessary.)

Do-It-Yourself Student Writing Sample

Use this blank form to create your own Student Writing Sample prompt.

Prompt for a Writing Sample

Student Writing Sample

Name _____ Date _____

Writing Situation

Directions for Writing

_____

_____

_____

_____

_____

_____

_____

_____

_____

_____

_____

_____

_____

_____

Do-It-Yourself Rubric

Use this blank form to create your own scoring rubric for a writing sample.

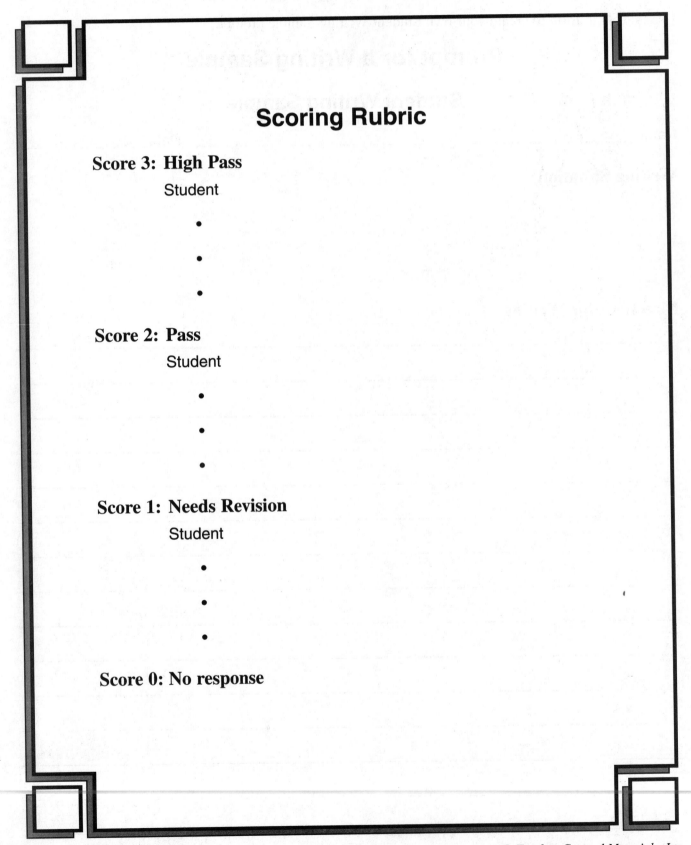

Scoring Rubric

Score 3: High Pass
Student

-
-
-

Score 2: Pass
Student

-
-
-

Score 1: Needs Revision
Student

-
-
-

Score 0: No response